bush
PUBLISHING
& associates

War of the World, Flesh, and the Devil

Copyright

All Scripture quotations are taken from the *King James Version* of the Holy Bible.

Boldface type indicates author's emphasis.

Attribution to other authors is given where known.
Notification of any omission will initiate a correction.

War of the World, Flesh, and the Devil

ISBN: 978-1-7329751-0-1
Copyright ©2019 David Keklikian

Bush Publishing & Associates, LLC., books may be ordered everywhere and on Amazon.com

For further information, please contact:
Bush Publishing & Associates   www.bushpublishing.com

Printed in the United States of America.

No portion of this book may be used or reproduced by any means: graphic, electronic or mechanical, including photocopying, recording, taping, or by any information storage retrieval system, without the written permission of the publisher, except in the case of brief quotations embodied in critical articles and reviews.

DEDICATED

TO THE

LIFE, LEGACY, BEAUTY, AND LOYALTY

OF

NANCY E. KEKLIKIAN

Faithful Wife, Mother, Grandmother
Escorted into Paradise January 22, 2016

ACKNOWLEDGMENTS

It is my privilege to pay tribute and thank the many who became a special part of my life during this writing. Prominent pillars will shine illustrious as their vivid testimonies reveal the outlandish truth in this hair-raising manuscript.

Other folks also have been a strength to mind, body, and soul while this book trilogy was long being wrestled to its battle-scarred completion.

My past and present personal family of righteous heritage has mentored me in the give-and-take art of loving, giving, receiving, and tenacity to a task. Their computer and technical helps were vital to the defeat of frustrations due to ignorance. Direct helps were given by my son **John**, and daughter **Deana (Spyres)**, and grandson **Riley Spyres**. Grandchildren remain an inspiration by their love and manifest gifts in theatre and music - **Jackson, Gigi,** and one-year-old, marvelous **Milo**. Deana edited and proofread the manuscript, helped Riley design the cover, and authored the book INFIDELITY. She also founded InSpyred *Images* – a premier video/photography company in Tulsa.

Philip Mark Keklikian – my faithful and dedicated brother – constant contributor, supportive prayer warrior, and ministry director – and I are recent widowers in regular contact.

First editor **Terry Lea** - transcribed tapes, edited and reorganized my massive pile of script into *"at least three books"*.

This small army nudged my character toward biblical standards demanded of this manuscript's readers. The result is provocative literature being read by millions, fulfilling pungent prophecy by **Evangelist Ray Bloomfield**, on March 13, 1965.

Special thanks to the staff at Village Inn Restaurants for excellent service during the writing of three manuscripts: **Managers** Danny Cochran, Raymond Montoya, Eric Fuller, Josh Sizemore.

Supervisors Laura Hackathorn, Stacey Blackwell, and Amy Boudreau; **Servers** Ayla Jones, Hannah Brown, Mindy Killman, Vanessa Barrios, Brenda and Maria Saldivar; Kris Soden, Jewel Mullins, Chris Ballard - **Cooks, Servicers**, et al – too many to name. May the Lord's blessings rest upon you.

TABLE OF CONTENTS

UP FRONT xiii
PREFACE xvii
CHAPTER 1: MAJOR DELIVERANCE CASES 1
    PATTY BATTLES 50 DEMONS 1
    PATTY'S BIOGRAPHY 37
CHAPTER 2: DIVERSE DELIVERANCE CASES 39
    MISSIONARY NORMAN PARISH - GUATEMALA 39
    UNIVERSITY PRESIDENT, DR. NICK 58
CHAPTER 3: AUTHOR'S BIOGRAPHY 69
    UPDATE ON PATTY 71
    HARD THINGS OF GOD 74
    OUR ENABLING AND GIFTING 79
    EXAMPLE OF CHANGE 80
    TEST OF OBEDIENCE 81
    LAUNCH INTO MINISTRY 85
    CATALYST FOR CHANGE 87
    PREPARATION BY DIVINE APPOINTMENT 91
CHAPTER 4: SIN AND ITS POWER 99
    ARMAGEDDON OF THE FLESH 105
CHAPTER 5: WARFARE DECREE 109
    DECREE FOR FAMILY AND PROPERTY 109
    DECREE FOR HOUSE AND HOUSEHOLD 110
    IT IS FURTHER DECREED: 111
CHAPTER 6: COINCIDENCE IS NOT BIBLICAL 115
    AUTHENTIC VS. FAKE MIRACLES 119
    FALSE ACCUSATION 119
    DEMONS AND JESUS KNOW EACH OTHER 120
    DISPOSITION AND RELOCATION OF EVICTED DEMONS 121
    TWO THOUSAND DEMONS IN ONE MAN 122
    WAYS IN WHICH THE LORD BRINGS DELIVERANCE 122

PHYSICAL ASPECTS OF DELIVERANCE *126*
LAYING ON OF HANDS *127*
PRACTICAL DISCERNING *133*
DEMONS MADE VISIBLE *136*

CHAPTER 7: PREPARATION AND DELIVERANCE **143**
AUTHENTIC VS. FAKE MIRACLES *143*
GIVING RIGHTS TO SATAN *144*
WHAT ARE ABOMINATIONS TO THE LORD? *144*
HOW EVIL SPIRITS GAIN ACCESS TO A CHRISTIAN'S LIFE: *147*
INDICATIONS OF DEMON PRESENCE *149*
PSYCHOLOGICAL SYMPTOMS *150*
RELIGIOUS SYMPTOMS *151*
ENSLAVING HABITS: *153*
PHYSICAL SYMPTOMS: *153*

CHAPTER 8: DELIVERANCE PROCESS AND EXAMPLES **155**
KNOW YOUR AUTHORITY *155*
SPEAKING THE WORD *161*
FORGIVENESS *162*
ASK, SEEK, KNOCK *165*
PRAYER AND FASTING *165*
CONFESS AND REPENT *168*
DISCERNING THE SPIRITS *168*
BIND AND LOOSE *174*

CHAPTER 9: WHAT TO EXPECT AND HOW TO RECEIVE YOUR DELIVERANCE **177**
PRACTICAL PREPARATIONS *180*
WHAT TO EXPECT AND HOW TO RECEIVE DELIVERANCE *182*
MINISTER'S PRAYER *184*
CANDIDATE'S PRAYER *184*
MINISTER'S INSTRUCTION: *187*

CHAPTER 10: INTERVIEW QUESTIONS AND ANSWERS **189**

UP FRONT

Thousands of hours had been expended in researching, writing, and editing this three-volume manuscript. I had just vocalized my love to the Lord in private worship. Suddenly, the question appeared in my mind in an unmistakable way: **"Would you let the Lord Jesus read this book?"**

Abashed, my mind now had to look carefully before answering. Surely there were imperfections – no doubt a few fleshly exaggerations … examples not properly detailed … perhaps a few personal prejudices had crept in … a veiled criticism of another ministry, and so forth. All these thoughts and more alerted me to reconsider all that had been written in support of my thesis. The Scripture then flashed into my mind: "Be ye therefore perfect as your Father in heaven is perfect" (Matthew 5:48). The feeling of dread came over me –

"I may have to throw it all away and start over. There goes four years of my life and dedication. I don't have the will, the strength, or enough time to begin again. There had been cash costs also - $12,000 - paid to one editor, and thousands more in peripheral expenses. It was already well over the budget of an unemployed widower eleven years retired.

On top of that, my promise to friends that they would receive my autographed gift-book, would have to be broken, branding me as a foolhardy liar.

My reply to the Lord's question was purposely being held in abeyance. I did not want to be snared by hastily spoken words or promises. After all, within a few moments of divine time I would have to answer for every word. "It is a fearful thing to fall into the hands of the living God" (Hebrews 10:31). Pondering the matter honestly, I began to reason with the Lord as this entreaty appeared: "Come now, and let us reason together, saith the Lord …" (Isaiah 1:18)

With these qualifying Scripture voices laid down, I was soon ready to reply:

"Lord, throughout the manuscript I have quoted your own words; they are perfect and shall never pass away. Neither of us can throw them out or change any part of them. Will you kindly be pleased to read them for yourself?". As for my words, they are not perfect in any respect – neither in grammar, punctuation, interpretation, presentation, or fact. No matter how many times I re-edit, I cannot make them perfect. This I know.

"In this understanding, and with your forbearance, my answer is, **'Yes, you may read this book.** Please be merciful in your forgiving laughter. Look upon my heart and not upon the outward appearance. Amen."

At once humbling and exhilarating, my spirit leaped for joy, putting a permanent smile in my soul. I hope you can see the gentle sweetness of the Lord asking my permission. In it he opened the gate a bit to see into heaven's loving, conversational relationships that we shall enjoy with him and the redeemed forever. Right here I need to shout Hallelujah!

It is in this same spirit that I proceed to publish. As reader and judge, your forbearance also is solicited in like manner as here requested of the Lord.

PREFACE

On the day this introduction was written I turned on the television and, by chance the 1959 science fiction film *Invisible Invaders* was showing. Its story line is: "A man learns of a plot to invade earth through the dead". The first dialog I heard was, "If we can't see them, we can't fight them." That was sufficient for me to continue watching. I thought, "How real that is. Humans indeed are dead in trespasses and sins, only because invisible Satan and his demons have invaded and instigated death on earth."

In another scene laboratory experiments revealed that the aliens could be made visible and be neutralized by soundwaves emitted from a sound-gun. The commander urgently asked the pious lady, "How fast can we reproduce this weapon? And if you have any special prayers for a mission like this, you better start praying! We only have enough oxygen for 90 minutes!"

That production was the unwitting precursor of the literal battle revealed in this manuscript fifty- nine years later! Our version of the "sound-gun" is our mouth that emits commanding sound-blasts in Jesus' name to "…destroy the works of the devil". The parallel applies even in the question: 'How fast can we reproduce this weapon?' To provide the answer to that question has been the driving force in writing this book.

Populations are indeed being destroyed through chaotic wars, famine, natural disasters, and individual turmoil of every kind. Newscasters loudly lament the ever-increasing carnage but offer no explanation or remedy. Governments likewise are stymied. Moreover, few spiritual leaders pinpoint the real cause. Yet, Jesus Christ and Apostles Paul and John warned that all categories of calamity would increase exponentially in the latter times (Matthew 24; and 2 Timothy 3:1-7). John 10:10 tells us: "The thief [Satan and his demons] cometh not but for to steal, and to kill, and to destroy." These are not idle words.

The very events there described are arriving in greater severity and frequency. Bible prophecy always comes to pass in exact detail. High profile teachers Irvin Baxter and Billy Crone are sounding an alarm through literature, television, internet, and audio-visual media to all populations. They document astounding sophistication of existing, unmanned, little known "Micro Aerial Vehicles" and "Swarm Technology of Micro Insects", at once remotely controllable worldwide through Artificial Intelligence. Civilian and military sectors of modern governments are racing to widen their capabilities for commerce and more lethal warfare. One said, "Developers are becoming afraid of their own inventions." They warn us to prepare for the comprehensive, imminent, and ominous happenings detailed in Scripture and documented in their "180 evidence clips".

The cause of this highly charged atmosphere is revealed in considerable detail through our personally experienced examples of satanic intrusions, which fortunately were defeated in battle! The testimony of Missionary Norman Parish, of Guatemala, presents his successful warfare against Satan's networking which has melded with ours. These and others together highlight the accelerating pace at which demonic assaults are plaguing individuals and nations everywhere.

There is no other reason for this book to exist apart from exposing little known facts and alerting believers to make right decisions with haste and to take appropriate action. Miraculous deliverances first recorded in the Holy Bible and now in these pages are to be replicated by ordinary believers as an undeniable witness to bible truth. The question that devout Jews had put to Peter in Acts 2:37 comes to mind: "Men and brethren, what shall we do?" The answer is always the same:

John the Baptist – Repent!

Jesus Christ – Repent!

Apostle Peter – Repent!

Repentance is integral to the gospel. How marvelously that message was preached in 1967 by long-time associate and friend, evangelist Raymond H. Bloomfield, of New Zealand. It is titled, "The Abiding Word and the Passing Voice". His message proclaims that the Word abides. And while the messenger's voice may quickly be snuffed out, it shall forever be shouted anew by an endless succession of inspired voices. Repent how? The late evangelist, David Wilkerson presented his solution. He said, "More than once I have been convicted of my sins against the very message I was preaching, even while preaching it." To confirm his message, he repented.

Would this not be a proper approach for today? The Holy Spirit stands ready to speak repentance to a preacher – even while he is preaching. What a wonderful blessing it will be for congregations to see leaders exemplifying their exciting, new and improved message ... the one of repentance and deliverance!

The two-fold problem of ignoring the devil and his agents is, first, it gives them enormous advantage to "steal, kill, and destroy" with near impunity. How shall "Thy will be done on earth as it is in heaven" be done on earth when co-regents of earth fail to obey our Father in heaven? Second, congregations lose their fear of the Lord when observing their leaders' low regard of the Lord's command to cast out demons [Mark 16:17]. Would-be victors are thereby left to remain captive.

With all diligence this costly message of love first had to be long lived before it could be authoritatively synthesized for reading. It is my prayer that God will use it to bring deliverance to those sick and suffering under pressures of everyday living. May it bring light, comfort, and the will to fight for release by those addicted to diverse bondages. May it stimulate leaders to correctively examine their messages, which may long have been devoid of repentance and deliverance. May the original gospel again be demonstrated as a battle cry, ascribing its due gravity and sobriety to people everywhere. Amen.

1

MAJOR DELIVERANCE CASES

PATTY BATTLES 50 DEMONS

What follows is the account and actual dialog - as close as handwritten notes could record - of a deliverance ministry to a Christian lady we will call Patty. Twelve eyewitnesses participated.
* The date: July 8, 1965.
* The place: second floor ballroom of the Chicago Conrad-Hilton Hotel.
* The event: the last afternoon session of the annual Full Gospel Businessmen's Fellowship International Convention

I am one of two men unknown to each other or anyone else in attendance, taking notes. We sat side-by-side, observing every detail of the event only three feet from the subject, soon to be drawn to participate in the urgent prayers of this incredible event. Accuracy of the dialogue was later verified between us and the minister. Explanatory comments are added where deemed appropriate.

Though unsophisticated in assessing spiritual matters at the time, my personal knowledge was massively increased through this episode, and later as a student under Derek Prince the next two years, and finally as an active deliverance minister during the next four decades. It is from the latter perspective that my comments are offered. Also, my systematic six-part teaching seminar titled, "The World of Spirits", is presented in another section. It opens texts of the Holy Bible on this subject, as well as drawing upon my personal work in dozens of exorcisms. Together these confirm the truth of modern-day biblical deliverance from demons who indwell multitudes of individuals, including Christians.

Keep in mind that all the 50 + demons named here and cast out of Patty- and millions more, for that matter - are still alive and actively seeking humans to torment. That is their job and they do it with diligence. Doubtless, some of them have been harassing you. Why else would you be attracted to read a book on this subject? Demons do not die. They merely change their address after being evicted. That is what bad tenants always do. You are one of their ongoing targets if you are a true Christian. Are you prepared to deal with them? Surely you will identify with some of their vexations in reading the following pages.

To someone unfamiliar in this subject the facts presented could raise concerns and fear of what implications there may be for you personally. Please set that aside. A born-again Christian is vastly superior to a demon in every way, and the demons know it. They fear *you*, especially when you learn of their cowering weakness and resounding defeats in every case detailed in this book. This fact makes it all the more important for you to learn of your power over them. Such knowledge not only protects you from their wiles, it helps prepare you to become an effective deliverance minister by making your faith to soar! Never fear demons or their bluffs.

Let us begin the telling:

Derek Prince was the primary conference teacher five afternoons, explaining the "Hindrances to Fullness of the Holy Spirit". The last two sessions emphasized the presence of evil spirits. At the close of the last day Reverend Prince made an altar call for those who felt they needed deliverance prayer.

Nearly 200 people came forward from the audience estimated at 600! During the authoritative prayer time there were many deliverances with outward manifestations. An unforgettable one was a Puerto Rican woman who hissed like a serpent while slithering across the floor in true serpentine fashion before her freedom was won. At the moment I was shocked, but later was grateful to have witnessed such a spectacle under the tutelage of Derek Prince. It prepared me for a day one year later when another lady, named Dixie, also slithered on the floor hissing as a serpent at the feet of my wife and myself, literally under the chair in front of ours. Soon we became well acquainted as friends in fellowship and corresponded when she enrolled in an out-of-state Bible Institute. Yet, none was so startling as that of Patty, which is the primary subject of this report.

It took five and a half hours for 50+ demons to reveal themselves, give their names, and be routed - screaming, crying, and convulsing. Many bowed before the name of Jesus upon command and confessed much about themselves before they were forced to depart from her. The deliverance concluded at 11:30 that night.

Present were Rev. Derek Prince and wife, Lydia; Mrs. Russell Meade, wife of Patty's pastor (Mrs. Meade had accompanied Patty to the meeting.); Rudy Roth, who also made written notes; Mr. & Mrs. Blaine and Helen Amburgy – prominent in the homebuilding industry; widely known new car dealer Bill Swad, from Columbus, Ohio; Cas Knoester, my future friend and associate from the nation of Holland, soon to be sent as missionary to Kenya; unnamed president of the Aurora, Illinois Chapter of Full Gospel Businessmen's Fellowship; and myself, business executive at the time; in addition to one or two others not known to me.

Entering the auditorium, I was startled to hear protracted, blood-curdling, screams coming from the center of the room - diabolic to be sure, yet beyond understanding. My purpose had been to find a quiet room and meditate while reading my new, red leather-bound Kirkbride Bible. Reverend Oral Roberts was scheduled to preach in another auditorium.

I saw the backside of a lady sitting alone, her head bent down. About 50 feet in front of her sat another woman facing Derek and Lydia Prince, who were standing before her. We five were the only people in the ballroom amid a thousand empty chairs in neat rows.

As the Princes were exorcising a spirit of witchcraft from the lady in front of them, a demon in the nearer lady began manifesting himself in screams. These were the sights and sounds as I entered the room!

The same kind of demon in the nearer lady was also at work in the other woman, whom the Princes were challenging! It is noteworthy that multiple demons have the same assigned roles and corresponding character traits for each demon name. While they are present wherever humans live, none is omnipresent, but they often travel great distances unhindered. In this particular case, the screaming demon in the nearby lady was attempting to provide relief to the first by screaming to distract his minister oppressor. The latter spirit was in distress by reason of the Derek Prince commands for him to depart. The screamer was, militarily speaking, drawing fire away from his partner.

Demons bring strength to one another in close proximity - two comprising more combined strength than one alone - an established biblical principle. While that effort succeeded in helping the one, it was "fatal" to the other, because the helper and cohorts were soon cast out, losing their covert residence.

I had not fully entered into the auditorium but stood at the open doorway observing these demonic antics. I wondered whether it was safe to enter and considered going back into the hallway to rethink the matter. In the Hollywood movie business, I was well acquainted with horror films in which actors screamed convincingly; but this was not Hollywood, and there was no camera crew. This was the real deal and my curiosity rose even higher than my adrenalin rush. Proceeding cautiously, I chose a seat at a safe distance from the disturbance yet close enough to observe the freakish scene. I could move out of the way if things started flying and make a hasty exit at the slightest threat. Keep in mind, this was the South side of Chicago, where the ironic made headlines - and, who knew whether this might become another bloody news event!

The eyewitnesses named above began arriving one and two at a time - the first being Rudy Roth, an elevator operator, with note pad in hand. He would soon sit beside me, likewise awed and curious, to observe this anomaly. Eyes wide-open, I sat there thinking, "This would make a terrific horror movie - fiction or not!

Rev. Derek Prince and his wife, Lydia, left the first woman and approached the screamer. After briefly talking to Patty, they began praying. Almost immediately, six sharply enunciated names began spewing out of Patty's mouth, like a roll call. These were not gentle female voices one might expect from a slender, attractive lady of 32 years age, but rather the marshaled, raspy, guttural voices of demons.

The names were not of the kind by which humans are usually identified. The demon voices were loud and proud:

"I'm Witchcraft! She will be a medium". "I'm a sorcerer!" Then, "Torment!" "Divination!"

"Deceitfulness!" "Shame!"

It is uncertain whether all names were spoken by one voice. But they really got my attention!

The battle was on, and suddenly, there was a new, strong male voice: "Religious Bondage! I am strong!"

Reverend Prince responded with authority, "No you are not strong! You were defeated at Calvary! Satan, in the name of Jesus, you're coming out!"

Demon: "No, I will not. I cling!"

Derek Prince: "Yes, you WILL come out in the name of Jesus!"

Patty, following Rev. Prince's instruction, declares, "The Blood of Jesus cleanses me."

Prince, in agreement with Patty: "Through the Blood of Jesus you will come out. I cast you out in the name of Jesus Christ!"

At this point, Prince admonished all present to pray: "The need is real prayer. This is a terrible struggle, a real battle." The praying became louder and more vehement.

Suddenly I found myself becoming an enthusiastic participant, as though part of a zany movie script. Astonishing - unlike any reality I had known. Here were actual combative, hostile conversations between invisible beings inside a young woman, and authoritative human adults. Can this be real? Who would believe this?

The battle continued…

Demon: "I am SORRY."

Prince: "Get out, Satan; I am not the least bit sorry for you! Get out of this body! Get out of this building! Come out in the name of Jesus! In the name of Jesus Christ, get out now!"

Demon: "I'm Lonely!"

Prince: "It's time you come out now, in Jesus' name!"

Demon: "Oh, P -L -E -A -S -E!"

The voice was diminished and weak, as if imploring for mercy and begging us to stop.

Prince: "Bag and baggage, you must be removed!"

Several spirits have left by this time, but there are more.

Prince commands: "What's your name? In Jesus' name, answer me!"

Demon: "Stubbornness and Pride. I don't get out easily!"

Prince: "Oh, yes …you …will! Come out now!"

Demon: "I get stubborn now!"

Prince wields the Word of God as a sword, referenced as such in 1 Samuel 15:23, to exert pressure: "Stubbornness is as the sin of witchcraft and idolatry!" then commands, "You come right out through the Blood of Jesus!"

With throat retching, coughing, and screaming, this spirit pair departed. And then…

Demon: "Fear of the Future. I fear the future."
Prince: "Come on, loose her! Come out of her in Jesus' name!"

Patty is instructed to pray a specific prayer, as clear evidence to Satan and to the Lord that she desired to be on legal ground with her Lord and Savior.

Patty: "Lord, please forgive my sins. Wash me in your precious Blood."
Prince: "If there is another spirit, manifest yourself!"

More of the terrible demonic screams ensued.

Prince: "OUT! Every last remaining presence of Satan come out! Out you must come!
Prince instructs Patty: "Now, I want you to repeat after me, 'I am cleansed by the Blood. I am redeemed by the Blood of Jesus. The Blood of Jesus cleanses me.'"

Eager to cooperate, Patty carefully repeats each phrase as it is given.

Prince: "Now, get out, in the name of Jesus!"

Surprisingly, a series of religious spirits suddenly came forward to identify themselves.

The next spirit names himself:

> Demon: "I'm Seducer of the Faith - Seducing. I am the main one!
>
> Demon: "Seduction and Error. I have many roots!"
>
> Prince: "You sneaky, seducing spirit, come out! The Blood of Jesus is against you. You seducing spirit, you strong one, you spirit of error - out! God's truth is against you. She acknowledged the truth. Jesus Christ IS the truth. Every one of your roots, come out. Every root of error and false teaching, OUT!"

Again, the spirit goes out with retching, coughing, and screaming, making place for departure of the next one, who is ordered to name himself.

> Demon: "I am Eternal Security. I believe it!"

This demon of Eternal Security quotes and misapplies scriptures, then misquotes other scriptures before being forced to vacate. This began a parade of some 37 cult spirits who proudly identified themselves by name in an unexpected sequential cadence. Though some departed, none left voluntarily. They were forcibly expelled under duress, by command of the superior authority, which is ours. Some proclaimed their beliefs or where they came from before being expelled:

Demon: "I am Free Grace!"

Prince: "You come out!"

Demon: "I am British Israel. Judgment is waiting!"

Demon: "I am Jesus-Only!"

Demon: "I am Manifested Sons of God!"

Demon: "Mormon! I'm from Salt Lake City."

Prince: "You Mormon spirit, come OUT of her!"

Demon: "Theosophy."

Demon: "Witchcraft - Falsehood."

Again, in response to instructions, Patty declares, "I loose myself from Witchcraft, Divination, and every spirit of the occult, in Jesus' name."

Prince "What kind of falsehood?"

The reply was not heard, but the spirit was expelled.

Prince: "All demonic forces come out - right out, now!"

Demon: "Metaphysics!"

Demon: "Seventh Day Adventist. I live right -I don't drink coffee!"

Demon: "Rosicrucian!"

Demon: "Star of Bethlehem - the Order!"

Demon: "I am Baha'i!"

Demon: "False Prophecy! I come from Mrs. Hale's teaching, in Toronto."

Demon: "I am Modern. I don't believe in Blood - not necessary today!"

Prince: "You spirit that denies the Blood, come OUT!"

Demon: "I am Jewish Orthodox. I'm better than you! I've got more money than you."

Demon: "Humanism. No religion - I'm just plain good! HA! HA! HA! I'm just humanist. I am the last root."

Demon: "Rosary. Hail Mary! Hail Mary! Mother of Peace, Mother of Grace, Mother of God. Purgatory!"

In 1 Timothy 2:5 it is stated: "For there is one God, and one mediator between God and men, the man Christ Jesus." That excludes any other mediators, such as living or deceased humans, spirits, or angels, (Revelation 22:8-9). Obeisance to idols and images is forbidden, referencing Exodus 23:24; 34:13-14. In the Gospel of Matthew, chapter 4:10b, Jesus restates it as: "Thou shalt worship the Lord thy God, and Him only shalt thou serve." Thus, we are instructed not to bow before, pray to, neither worship, nor serve any other than the Creator, the Lord Jesus Christ, forbidding any form or style of worship of idols, images, or their apparitions.

A follow-on is that Mary, the virtuous virgin, magnificent mother of Jesus, knew that every human is born a sinner in need of salvation from sin's penalty. For at Luke 1:47 Mary declared that her spirit "rejoiced in God my Saviour". According to Scripture, only sinners who have been redeemed through forgiveness of their sin could rightly say, "my Saviour". In Luke 11:2-4 Jesus taught us to pray, "Our Father ...", not mother. In the case here reported, the demon named himself and his false doctrine by praying, "Hail Mary, Hail

Mary! Mother of Peace, Mother of Grace, Mother of God." He was in three ways exposed as a liar: 1. He was not the lady Mary, 2. not a mother of either grace or of God, and 3. His worship was not to the God of creation, as required by Jesus. A total fraud, he was summarily cast out of his victim, and shall ultimately be cast into hell with his father the devil.

Continuing with Patty's deliverance, the next spirit identified himself and his teaching:

Demon: "Soul Sleep, and I am tired. No punishment."
Prince asks: What more can you tell us?
Demon replies: "I'm from Liverpool, England!
Demon: "Asceticism! I'm from India."
Demon: "Yoga!"
Demon: "Mohammedan - Far East; India - All over. I'm taking over!"
Demon: "Snake Worship!"
Demon: "Pentecost – Zion - Jerusalem!"

This demon's assumed name may seem confusing, but when an evil spirit calls himself 'Pentecost' his work is to falsify, mock, and cause doubt, because Pentecost is a true biblical feast day as well as identifying the miraculous outpouring and empowering of the Holy Spirit (See Acts 2:1-3). Further, there is an evil spirit who induces "False Tongues" as relates to Pentecost. One such has spoken to me in California, as explained in another case. There cannot be a "false" without a "true".

Something astounding has unfolded here. I want to emphasize it so that Christian readers may realize its implications. These demons are claiming to be fully engaged and operational in and from all parts of the world: Canada, England, India, the Far East, Israel; The United States, and East Africa. Add Mexico, Guatemala, El Salvador, Central America, as shown in a following report. It appears these alien invaders have made it unsafe for everyone on earth. Not only are they on every populated continent, but collectively they seem to know something about everything and everyone in our culture! Though essentially overlooked, this fact should have been obvious because the Holy Bible was written to enlighten humanity everywhere as to the battle between good and evil. (NASA might want to change its focus on aliens in outer space to those on planet earth!). So also, might the leaders of the Christian church at large. Many believers wonder why leaders avoid the deliverance accounts and admonitions emblazoned on so many pages of the Holy Bible.

MAJOR DELIVERANCE CASES

Let us now look at an excerpt taken from the next pages of testimony of my friend, Missionary to Guatemala, Norman Parish. It pertains to the worldwide network of Satan's forces, as stated above.

Page 2: "In Guatemala – a country of four million people – there were over 1000 centers where witchcraft, sorcery, and spiritism were practiced. As the evil spirits left the bodies and minds of people who had been bound, they (the demons) returned to their centers to report what had happened to them. The human agents of Satan – witchdoctors, Spiritists, and mediums – became terribly troubled and began to dispatch more demons to work against us."

Page 8: "It was revealed that there were 21 such major spirit centers in Mexico, Guatemala, and El Salvador working against us, all at the same time. We became sick – the oppression so great that we suffered both bodily and mentally. We discovered the depths of Satan's power and Satan's work. We actually went behind the veil and saw how Satan operates. The devil revealed who he was: 'I am the Prince of Guatemala and surrounding territory. I am Satan. I am the overlord of this whole area of the world'. The boy's covenant (the teenager being delivered) had been made with the powers that were over that whole area – a principality."

For clarity and emphasis, here is the recap of nations and continents identified by the demons in just these two reports, where high level and low-level demons have operated.

NATION	**CONTINENT**
Jerusalem, Israel	Middle East
Mohammedan (Province)	Asia - Middle East
India	Greater Asia
Mexico	Central America
Guatemala	Central America
El Salvador	Central America
Canada	North America
United States of America	North America
England (Liverpool)	Europe
Kenya (Manduri)	Africa
"All Over"	Everywhere

Another account references Italy, Germany, and Russia. From these accounts we learn that demons are multi-lingual and have for centuries lived among us, on, and inside of individuals of all cultures and geographic locations. From the beginning they have been familiarizing themselves with our inner workings - their mission being first to influence, then to destroy organs, tissue, nerves, skeleton, mind, emotions, and finally our very lives. It began with our genesis in "… a garden eastward in Eden", where Satan was with Eve and Adam. Perhaps you have read the account in the first three chapters of the Holy Bible. Even so – apart from pre-law pagans - it has been fairly rare that a human in the civilized world becomes so totally overtaken as to be an uncontrollable demoniac. Dictators and other individual mass murderers, however, have been thus taken over and driven to commit heinous crimes on a massive scale.

Demons externally interact with governmental and societal structures through elected or dictatorial leaders. At least in part, that is why we are told to pray for our leaders and magistrates (1 Timothy 2:1-2), "… that we might lead a quiet and peaceful life in all godliness." Oftentimes a demon has inhabited a baby in the mother's womb and wreaked havoc an entire lifetime until his victim either dies a natural death or is killed by him.

Humans die, and their body is removed from activity on earth, while demons have no body and remain evil spirits on earth after being cast out. This means that their population has never been reduced. Upon the death of a human victim any resident evil spirit is released to find another victim. It is well to keep in mind that the Lord has placed restraints upon them, so that they must find justifiable grounds and ways to enter, which are many. Their ways and means of entry are clearly explained in chapters of our seminar, transcribed to become part of this series of books. All are under the general heading of The World of Spirits. In spite of the foregoing negatives revealed, we are not to fear Satan. Quite to the contrary, he and they fear us, once we are enlightened of their workings.

Multiply the above facts by millions of humans of every generation over 6000 years. Does it not seem incredible that an unbroken chain of otherworldly spirit beings resides alongside our spirit and soul, and in uncountable cases, inside our body? Yet, numerous Scriptures prove it to be true. I am not saying everyone is infested with demons, but, as Derek Prince said more than once, "I wouldn't issue a demon-free certificate to anyone." Neither would I. But it would be dangerously presumptuous to merely assume we are free of demonic influence.

The next spirit to speak in response to Derek Prince's command was:

Demon: "POLTERGEIST!"
Demon: "Fetish! I worship god in the trees and rocks. I have seen you in East Africa!"
Prince: "I don't want just that information - that's an area. Tell us more. What part of East Africa?"
Demon: "The barren country--Manduri. I followed you all over!"

Prince lived in Kenya, East Africa five years as principal of a missionary school. He was the only person in the room this day who understood the African language the demon was speaking. Prince then tested this spirit because, at first, it began answering questions in Swahili. To my amazement, Prince commanded him to speak in English! First, he wanted to prove whether this spirit was telling the truth. Second, he wanted to further educate us. He required the spirit to answer in English what he knew about an acquaintance of Reverend Prince in Kenya. The spirit replied that the man was a tribal chief who liked feathers. Then Prince asked the spirit to tell him about another man who also lived there. The other man worshiped trees.

The spirit answered correctly. In all, there were about five separate questions that no one else in the room could possibly have answered unless they had lived in Kenya. Reverend Prince affirmed to us that all answers from this spirit were true and accurate.

Having satisfactorily proved the veracity of his reply to Derek Prince, relative to Kenya, the demon said further, "I followed you all over." I heard him give answers in the two languages, both of which Prince knew and confirmed. I only understood his answers when he switched from Swahili to the English language.

Notice two things here: the demon was fluently bilingual and had traveled to different continents. Prince explained for the benefit of those present, the Lord was causing these spirits to reveal more information than they normally had to, and further explained that he rarely engaged in conversation with an evil spirit, other than to command him to depart.

Especially noteworthy was that they had for years known and literally followed Prince on foot so to speak, in Africa and Britain, and now in the United States. A demon in Patty told us he (the spirit) was from Liverpool, England - Prince's home country. Patty, herself a native of England, had relocated to Canada via the Liverpool Port, and later moved to the United States. Naturally, the accompanying demons either had motivated the moves, or, surreptitiously went along for the ride. Either way, at this meeting they again caught up with their prized target, Derek Prince.

We see here that the hierarchy of evil spirits had considered Rev. Prince enough of a threat to assign demon agents to track his every move in at least the three specified countries. It is certain they also followed him during his ministry in dozens of nations as he systematically taught the Bible to multitudes, cast out demons, and performed numerous miracles of other types. Being a high value target of the enemy is a compliment, which he well deserved. His more than 50 years of counseling and teaching was to peoples on all populated continents. He had lived 20 years in the Jerusalem he loved and raised his family there. Though he passed into eternity in 2003 at age 88, the spread of his teachings yet grows exponentially through books, audio-visual media, and the Internet.

Most informed Christians have learned something about the work of Satan and his demons. Jesus explained, "The thief cometh not, but for to steal, and to kill, and to destroy: I am come that they might have life, and that they might have it more abundantly" (John 10;10). While demons are assigned to specially target ministers who dare expose their hidden works of darkness, they cannot work under scrutiny because their lesser authority can be defeated when challenged by our greater authority in Jesus Christ. "Behold. I give unto you power to tread on serpents and scorpions [types of demons], and over all the power of the enemy: and nothing shall by any means hurt you (Luke 10:19).

Now let us continue with the rest of Patty's deliverance dialog:

Prince: What is your name?"
Next Demon: "DANCE IN CHURCH! I go to church - all the big meetings - A.A. Allen - Jesus Only - Tom Lowry. I like Allen's the best. He thinks I'm religious and from God."

During the 1940's, A.A. Allen was internationally known as a fiery evangelist who cast out demons. A Google or YouTube search might still provide actual video examples of Reverend Allen's deliverance work, though they could have been removed.

Demon: "I am RHYTHM. I come from the nightclub. I go to colored churches - they like rhythm. Baptist Church. I like the Fish Dance. I was at Teen Challenge" - all spoken in fast staccato.

Patty later revealed that she and a girlfriend had mimicked the then popular Fish Dance. In jest, she also had imitated certain homosexual expressions. Yet, just a mocking imitation gave those demons an opening to enter.

Notice the warnings in Ephesians 5:3-4. "But fornication, and all uncleanness, or covetousness, let it not be once named among you, as becometh saints; neither filthiness, nor foolish talking, nor jesting, which are not convenient: but rather giving of thanks." And in verse 12: "For it is a shame even to speak of those things which are done of them in secret." Satan is a legalist who takes advantage of those who foolishly disobey. Let us thereby be instructed.

> Demon: "Homosexual. I imitate."
> Prince: "You demon, come out. I know you, demon."
> Demon: "I know you know me!"
> Prince instructs Patty: "Renounce it yourself."
> Patty: "Homosexual spirit, I renounce you! The Blood of Jesus cleanses me from all my sins."

For renunciation to be effective it should be spoken audibly in the presence of a witness to complete the legal transaction. A second witness is like a notary's seal, which authenticates a document.

Considering the work of this demon, we call attention to the danger in American federal policy that has promoted acceptance of homosexual and trans-gender practices, even to the point of financing bizarre surgical procedures with money collected from taxpayers. Such bureaucratic coercion extends into federal prisons, all military branches, government institutions, and is promoted through public elementary school administrations all the way through colleges and universities. From a literal standpoint there is nothing gay, righteous, or wholesome in aberrant practices condemned by major religions of the world. Some of the instructive Scriptures are Genesis 19:24-25 and Romans 1:26-32.

Many of their practices are disease-prone, are demonically inspired, and, if not checked can lead to destruction of person and nation. As these Scriptures are the Words of God, their conclusion has nothing to do with any human's personal opinion. Arguments against the words must be taken up with God Himself. Even the god of the Muslim Quran fiercely condemns homosexual conduct and makes it punishable by death. These combined conclusions seem to confirm there is nothing wholesome about its practice.

Patty's deliverance continues:

Prince: "Who else is in there?"
Demon: "Masturbation - I'm NOT coming out! I have nowhere to go … Oh, I know! I'll go to the Playboy Club, I have a victim there!"
Prince: "That's a good place for you. Get out of this body - get out of this building! Come out in the name of Jesus. In the name of Jesus Christ, get out now!"

The Playboy Club was close to the scene of this event. Getting this spirit out required much struggle, as he had become deeply embedded a long time. Realize that this is an early stage homosexual act and should not be permitted to become habitual. Children will experiment. Sometimes a medical doctor will require it of a man to obtain a specimen for testing. There may be other valid reasons for it occasionally. Whatever the cause or purpose, be guarded for the reasons shown. Its bondage can be terrible in and of itself, but more destructively it opens the door for other demons to enter in to torment the individual.

> Prince to the next spirit: "Give me your name."
> Spirit #1: "I am Confusion. I won't come. No! I am not coming. I am confused."
> Spirit #2: "I am Restless."
> Spirit #3: "I am Dissatisfied - we belong together!"
> Prince: "Confusion, Dissatisfaction, Restlessness – you godless trio, come out!"
> Patty: "I loose myself from all three in the name of Jesus. The Blood of Jesus Christ cleanses me from all my sins."
> After struggling, the three spirits finally departed.
> Demon: "PAIN! PAIN! PAIN! Back Infirmity - Sciatica - Pain of the Nerves - Pain of the Vertebrae!"

There is natural pain, which by design alerts us to something wrong that needs our attention. Beyond that, there is often a supernatural pain induced by tormenting demons. Pain medication mitigates natural pain but has no effect on pain supernaturally induced. One effective help for both types is to speak aloud your resistance as in Isaiah 53:5 [fully translated] which shows that Jesus bore our "sickness and pains" in addition to our sins.

Prince: "You tormenting spirit of pain, come out of her. You demon of infirmity come out! All the medication to kill the pain, come out! Now, demon of pain, come out. Out you go – out in Jesus' name!

Patty, grimacing in agony, writhing from severe pain emanating from the low part of her back and down her legs - demons torturing and tearing her inner being - coughs, wretches, and regurgitates slimy habitations – partly a residue of pain medications - as the demons depart.

Deliverance is often accompanied by unpleasant physical regurgitations. Wisdom dictates that advance provision be made by having napkins, tissue, or paper towels and waste containers available when engaging demons in battle.

Prince: Who else is in there? Come on. Answer me!
Demon: "Death - I die slowly. I lurk in the hospital. I came from a dead body."

Patty had long worked as a registered nurse in a hospital and was still employed there.

Prince: "Whose dead body?"
Demon: "Brown - Mr. Brown. I'm death. I killed him - I'm death. I'll kill her!"
Prince: "Come out of this woman, you demon of death! Who else are you in?"

Demon: "I'm also in Pennie, Mrs. Sutherland, Herman Frazer, and Mike and Jo's baby."

Upon hearing the demon speak the names Mike and Jo, Patty became wide-eyed, and gasped. She knew this family very well and had lived with them. Suddenly realizing they could be in mortal danger, she told Prince that her friends had recently had a baby.

Is this not completely ironic? Patty had just heard the demon speak out of her own mouth to reveal for the first time, both to herself and to us, this shocking, deadly plan which the demon alone had kept secret from everyone! Do not let this point escape your understanding. I want to emphasize that this very demon of Death had a clear plan to commit two murders – that of Patty herself, and of her friends' baby. I want you to comprehend the irony.

Complete knowledge of the premeditated plan to commit murder was "inside" of Patty, but she did not know it. A proper question for a reporter to ask is, "What plans do they secretly have on the inside of you, about which you know nothing? Murder? Calamity? Either for you or for your family?" It is presumptuous to believe there are no such plans already underway and unfolding inside of you. Jesus clearly explained in John 10:10 that the "… thief cometh not, but for to steal, and to kill, and to destroy." Apostle Paul added in 1 Corinthians 10:13, "There hath no temptation taken you, but such as is common to man …".

Ever the opportunist, Satan does not make exceptions for you or for me. Jesus said the devil "... was a murderer from the beginning" (John 8:44). The satanic enemy will not openly reveal his murderous plots in advance. Nor will he let his host carrier know of his presence or even that he exists. Else it would be self-defeating. As we elaborate in later pages, his covert operatives, deceptions, and procedures are fully as "military" in character as are human armies. Our attempt here is to be a "code breaker", through which you may learn of their evil plans before they strike. This entails the study of how Satan operates through both demons and their collaborators – some openly, and others having been unwittingly infiltrated.

You see here that the exposé of the murderous plan was not volunteered. It came to light only when the demon was challenged and overpowered by superior authority – the Spirit of Christ working through the minister and us. Both the Holy and unholy spirits were resident inside Patty in this instance, both having full knowledge of the planned murder of the two individuals identified. The Lord spared them. We now continue with Patty's deliverance:

Prince: "Demon of Death, are you in anybody in this room?"

In response, the demon - now moving slowly and deliberately - peered hatefully through Patty's eyes, leaned forward, turned, and stopped to scrutinize each participant, one by one, glaring straight into our eyes, before passing to the next person. Having passed by me, he stopped, reversed direction, slowly turning back. He suddenly lifted Patty's arm, stretched it out stiffly and pointed her index finger directly at my eyes, and replied:

Demon: "HIM!" Then mockingly laughed with a smirk.
Prince: "What about him?"
Demon: "He's afraid of me."

Being confronted by Death, himself, right to my face caused my hair to bristle and muscles to tighten. It jarred me to wonder what it could mean. I had never before been directly threatened with death by a supernatural, invisible demon assassin! At the end of the session, Rev. Prince warned, "Brother, if I were you, I would take that very seriously!"

His warning justified my concern. Indeed, I was exceedingly careful driving home that night! The warning also solidified my stance of always being on guard. That wisdom seems to have paid off, because I am happy to report, Death did not triumph over me during the next 52 years. There were, however, eight near misses requiring miraculous interventions to save my life, and in one desperate episode, the lives of our entire family. The latest episode occurred while completing this manuscript for publication. I have come to see that Death can be deadly indeed!

Prince: "Now, Death, you come out of her in Jesus' name!" Then he instructed Patty, "You loose yourself and confess as follows: 'Death has no more dominion over me. You are a defeated enemy. Jesus defeated you on the Cross and rose from the grave." She fully complied in making that scriptural confession, phrase by phrase, which broke the demon's power to remain.

Demon: "I've lost her! I've lost her! I don't like you!"

Prince: "I don't like you either! You odor of death, you corruption, come out!"

The odor was horrible – far more than when caused by a "normal" throwing up. Exaggerated stench often occurs in deliverance, even when there is no regurgitation. Jesus referred to demons as "unclean" 18 times in the bible.

An example is found in Mark 1:23-27." There was in their synagogue a man with an unclean spirit; and he cried out, saying, 'Let us alone; what have we to do with thee, thou Jesus of Nazareth? Art thou come to destroy us? I know thee who thou art, the Holy One of God.' And Jesus rebuked him, saying, 'Hold thy peace, and come out of him.'

"And when the unclean spirit had torn him, and cried with a loud voice, he came out of him. And they were all amazed, insomuch that they questioned among themselves, saying, 'What thing is this? What new doctrine is this?' for with authority commandeth he even the unclean spirits, and they do obey him."

Surely it seems inappropriate and unfitting that, after 2000 years of Christian belief and practice, the reaction of witnesses remains "amazement", and the same questions are still being asked when these things happen.

Patty retched and regurgitated. It was dead quiet a moment. Rudy, the other note taker, wrote: "So quiet you could hear a pin drop."

Prince gives more scriptural confessions for Patty to make. One of the phrases was, "Jesus took the sting out of death." Patty complied word by word.

Prince: "All the poison, come out!" More regurgitating followed.

Patty further confesses: "Death has no more power over me in Jesus' name. Jesus is my Savior. By his blood, I am saved. Jesus is the Victor!"

Prince: "Every last vestige must go!"

Demon: "Oh, let me go!"

Prince: "I will not let you go - you must come OUT!"

Demon: "Somebody else want me? ANYBODY WANT ME ?!" Then plaintively appealed, "I want to rest in her a little."

Prince: "No, you come out. Listen to the name of Jesus!"

Demon: "I don't like it."

Prince instructs Patty: "Now, you testify openly."

She begins to testify. The demon dramatically torments her.

Prince: "The Blood of Jesus is against you. This is a temple of the Holy Spirit. Expire and come right out of her. Your power is broken.

The sixth of God's Ten Commandments is: "Thou shalt not kill [literally- do no murders]. Murder is the unjust killing of another human. A demon named Death is always and only a murderer. He incessantly kills humans by diverse premeditated plans, yet escapes punishment under the laws of man. Humans cannot bring an invisible, murdering demon to justice because human laws only apply to humans.

The law of God, however, has no such restriction. He alone shall bring demons to justice through eternal death in hell. The task for Christians is to discern a spirit of death inside a human and apply the only remedy available. That is, cast the demon out of his victim. Yes, the human murderer is also a victim, to the degree he is ignorant of the underlying compulsion to kill. Ignorant or not, however, he remains guilty of murder and is subject to its penalty.

Continuing here with Patty's deliverance, take notice that the demons throughout this engagement had to comply with the authoritative commands of a knowledgeable Christian. It is imperative that believers in Jesus Christ learn to know their superior authority over that of demons. See Luke 10: 17-21.

Prince: "Come on! I command you to tell me the truth! What is left?"

Demon, lilting and smirky: "I'm just a little PROUD."

Prince: "Come out of this woman, finally and forever!"

Patty: "The Blood of Jesus cleanses me. Every tormenting demon, go out of me!"

Prince: "We expel you finally and the last time!"

Demon: "I am Insanity."

Prince: "You demon of insanity, come out! Now, look at me. What kind of spirit are you?"

Demon: "Drug Addiction - tranquilizers!"

Prince: "Now, you demon of drug addiction, come out of her!"

Demon: "Sorrow - I'm so sorry. I SORROW! I SORROW! I SORROW! I'm s o r r e e y," apologetic and meek. "I'm so tired of sorrow and grief. It's so hard."

The demon in Patty's countenance and expression became pitiful - a depressing weeping spell ensued. Tears of self-pity flowed.

Demon: "I am Grief."

Prince: "Grief, come out."

After numerous demons were expelled, Patty was noticeably stronger and more assertive.

Patty firmly states: "I renounce you in the name of Jesus! I plead the precious Blood of Jesus" (to "plead," as when a lawyer pleads his case in a court of law).

Demon, speaking matter-of-factly: "Doubt - I am a spirit of Doubt."

Prince: Satan, you are a liar. I command you in the name of Jesus to come out."

Demon: "HEAVINESS."

Patty: "Heaviness, I renounce you!"

Demon: "I am harmless."

Prince: "No, you are NOT harmless. I command you to tell me..." [Deliverance note was not finished here.]

Isaiah 61:3 clearly identifies this demon as the "spirit of heaviness". It also shows that the remedy for it is offering praise to the Lord.

Demon: "Accusing. I accuse."

Prince: "Accusing demon, come out!"

Patty: "I am clean through the Blood of Jesus."

Prince: "Any more demons in there?"

Demon: "DEFEAT!"

Prince speaking to Patty: "Testify now."

Patty: "I loose myself from all defeat and discouragement."

Prince addressing the next demon: "What is your name?"

Demon: "Exhaustion."

Prince speaking to Patty: "Now testify."

Patty: "I resist all tiredness and weariness and fatigue. The Lord is my light and my strength. I loose myself from this weariness, in the name of Jesus."

Prince: "You bow and yield. You have to come out, in Jesus' name."

The demon bows Patty's head, and meekly comes out, as though truly weary, having no more energy to resist. Demons tire in battle just as we do, with a spiritual weariness that first may be feigned by the demon, but soon becomes literal for both the spirit and the minister.

Demon: "Obstruction! I obstruct the will of God."

Demon: "I'm Indecision! I'm fierce!"

Prince instructs Patty on a confession to make, which was:

Patty: "I resist you, Indecision. I want a sound mind. Depart from me."

Prince to next demon: "Look at me! What kind of spirit are you?"

Demon: "UNREST. I am coming out."

Demon goes out with a terrifying scream, offering no resistance.

Demon: "I am REBELLION!"

Prince: "You obey and get out!"

Lydia Prince addressing the spirit: "Now you look like a spoiled child."

The above embodies essential facts of this episode of deliverance but is by no means complete coverage. Printed pages cannot show the dramatic expressions in and through Patty's body and personality. Each demon expressed his own, unique, anti-Christ personality appropriate to his assignment.

Patty's facial expressions had changed with each expulsion, voices ranged from whimpering, to guttural, to feminine, to pitiful, to braggadocios many times over. Screams were voluminous among the retching, spitting of phlegm and other disgusting physical evidences of demonic habitations. Semi-violent physical reactions were seen throughout this five-and-a-half-hour struggle.

Even though the deliverance process was arduous and physically exhausting, when it ended, she happily said, "David, I feel light as a feather!" Joyous, jubilant, and smiling widely she repeated, "I can't get over how light I feel - as though I could float!" High in amazement, I rejoiced with her, while, at the same time envying her newfound freedom. I thought that what she had just received might be exactly what I needed, which soon proved to be true.

At the end of the main session, Patty removed herself and at a distance, continued praying in similar fashion with her pastor's wife, who had accompanied her to the meeting. Mrs. Meade was competent in the ministry - her husband having authored "Victory Over Demonism Today," an early and excellent book on deliverance. Other spirits not named above were then evicted.

Through the lengthy and arduous process, Patty, Mrs. Meade and all other participants were euphoric at the display of God's grace and revelation. Our faith was recharged by reliving the most neglected part of the New Testament narrative, and in learning how to be more effective in expelling demons. It was shown that, not only professional ministers, but also the laity are admonished and enabled to perform exorcisms, just as Jesus required of his first followers. His command has never been altered or rescinded: "And these signs shall follow them that believe: In my name shall they cast out devils [literally *demons*] ..." (Mark 16:17). That command carries no time limit or qualification, except that one must be a "believer" in Jesus Christ.

Prior to this event, Patty had become a formal student of the Bible, and graduated with a four-year degree. She remains Pentecostal in doctrine, persuasion, and experience, certainly not a novice in her Christian faith. Following this event, she and our family became good friends, fellowshipping in Chicago's Faith Tabernacle at the intersection of Grace Street and Broadway - "where grace meets the broad way!"

Before this deliverance, she had led an inwardly challenging Christian life, with an understandably high level of warfare between the "demonized" old nature and the new one free in Christ. Afterwards, she testified that life had become quite normal with less stress, yet required diligence to maintain the freedom gained. She has continued a devout walk with Christ and is known and respected by prominent Christians. Here marks the end of Patty's most major deliverance, though more was to come. Seven years were to pass before I would learn that she had experienced deliverance encounters prior to this one, though somewhat less extensive than the one reported here.

PATTY'S BIOGRAPHY

Patty was born and raised in England and was educated as a registered nurse. As a young adult she departed England from the port of Liverpool in a permanent move to Canada, where she received Christ in a Salvation Army meeting. She was baptized in the Holy Spirit in the church of Rev. Maxwell Whyte, a native Englander living in Canada. She worked as registered nurse sixty years – both in hospital and mobile, retiring in 2016. She graduated with a four-year degree from a Bible College in Illinois, was missionary to Mexico for six months. As this book was being readied for the publisher, we renewed fellowship with Patty by telephone and mail. She enthusiastically approved of our reporting on her deliverance and remains steadfast in Christian faith and practice.

2

DIVERSE DELIVERANCE CASES

MISSIONARY NORMAN PARISH - GUATEMALA
GRACE GOSPEL CHURCH, WACO, TEXAS 1964

When the Holy Spirit came upon us in the mission field in Guatemala, the only natural and honest thing to do was write the church and tell them all about it. We wrote a detailed six-page letter about the moving of the Spirit. We held nothing back. We thought it would be the end of our relationship with this Baptist church and denomination, thinking for sure they would kick us out.

Thank the Lord they have been very fair. So far, they have stood by us, backed us in our work, prayed and supported us.

They did become a little concerned about what was happening to us in the mission field: the gifts of the Spirit flowing and the wonderful wooing of God in healing and deliverance. So, they sent a pastor down, the writer of the Sunday School Lesson and the Sunday School Times, an outstanding speaker. He came down to Guatemala for a 12 days visit and saw everything that was going on. He saw the gifts of the Spirit in operation and the power of God being manifested through our believers and pastors. The day he was leaving I asked him, "Brother Fiest, what is your impression of the work?" He said, "Norman, I cannot agree or readily accept everything because of my degree and denominational background, yet the Spirit witnesses to my spirit that this is real." Since then the church has not only supported us but their interest has increased.

We were in Canada for a month to minister to a certain extent in a church there, but they never let me get behind the pulpit—never did let me preach. I think they were afraid. We were surprised and, in a sense, disappointed, but we had wonderful times of fellowship with the brethren. We had our own meetings in different homes, meeting anywhere from three to forty people at a time. It was in the home group meetings that we gave our testimony. We told about the work of the Holy Spirit and the way God had come down into our midst to deliver His people from the bondage of sin, sickness, and Satan.

The revival God gave Guatemala continued as 20 continuous months of heaven in two glorious years. We experienced the power and the love of God.

We must confess that we human beings have held God back. We interfered. We fumbled the job. We had so many weaknesses and failures that the revival did not grow or spread as much as we would have wanted. We thank God that He is merciful, in spite of ourselves and the way we acted.

The development of deliverance ministry was one of the outstanding gifts from our revival. We entered wholeheartedly into it, but it was not easy. It demanded 100% consecration and to a certain extent, sacrifice on our part. It demanded time, effort and strength, but it has been wonderful to see people brought from the power of Satan to the power of God, to see shackles broken, and people entering into glorious liberty as sons of God.

We were thrown into a battle against witchcraft and Spiritism. We never thought Guatemala would be so steeped in it. Guatemala is a Catholic country. They have a certain sense of Christianity, but we have discovered that in Guatemala—at the time a small country of four million people—there were over 1,000 centers where witchcraft, sorcery, and Spiritism were practiced. When we began to deal with cases of people oppressed or possessed of demons because of these occult centers, we were unconsciously thrown head long into battle with them. Why? Because as the evil spirits left the bodies and minds of the people who had been bound, they returned to the centers to report what had happened to them and talked about their defeat. The witchdoctors, Spiritists, and mediums became terribly troubled and began to dispatch demons to work against us. At times we experienced such great oppression that we knew those witchdoctors were confederating against us.

It was revealed that there were 21 such major spirit centers in Mexico, Guatemala, and El Salvador working against us at the same time. We were sick—the oppression so great that we suffered both bodily and mentally. You know, this is going to happen more and more in these last days. We must be ready. We must be sober. We must be vigilant for we know the battle against the forces of death and darkness—the kingdom of Satan—is going to increase greatly.

Let me tell you about one of the cases we had in Guatemala.

One Tuesday morning we were dealing with a woman who was under a curse of witchcraft when the Holy Spirit led me to go outside into the street. There I found a woman and a man looking up at our church building. I approached them and asked what they needed. They informed me they had just arrived from a town named Huehuetenango near the Mexican border. They had brought to the city their 16 years old son who had suddenly gone wild—lost his mind. They were bringing him to intern him in a mental institution for treatment. But when they arrived in the city and called the hospital, they were told they would have to wait, there was no bed available at the time. So, they took the boy to one of their relatives, a pastor of a Central American church whose mission is a fundamental mission, but they do not really believe in God's power to heal or deliver—at least they don't practice it. One of the neighbors had told them about our revival.

We had made no publicity about the revival. We didn't make a radio announcement or a bulletin. We thought it would be best to keep quiet; let the Lord make the publicity. When God is really working, you don't have to spend money on radio or print. The news gets around. It flies from mouth to mouth, home to home, and town to town. Though the neighbor lady did not belong to our church, she told them to get in touch with us. That's what they were seeking to do. It's why they had arrived at our church that Tuesday morning.

We felt led of the Lord to take this case under our responsibility. We usually didn't go to pray for people in their homes but in this case, something inspired us to go.

At two o'clock that afternoon I went to the house with two brethren who are anointed of the Spirit. As we went in the front door, the boy, who was in a backroom of the house and couldn't even see or hear us, began to shriek and writhe as the evil spirits that were in control began to manifest themselves.

The family became perturbed and didn't even want to let us in. They thought our presence would disturb him and create even more harm in this boy. After a while of discussion, we were able to persuade them to open the way. As we entered the room, this boy was in a pitiful state.

The leading of the Lord prompted me to sit at the edge of the bed. I didn't even talk to the boy. I sat down and addressed Satan. The boy was unconscious, in a trance. I said, "Satan, we come against you in the name of the Lord Jesus Christ in the authority that has been given unto us over all the power over the enemy. I command you to leave this body and release this boy!"

Suddenly, the boy sat up and began to talk. He started eating. He had been completely unconscious for a week—all his physical and mental functions had ceased. But he sat up, he recovered and seemed to be normal.

Following a time of prayer and praise we left that place. Still within my heart I knew the battle was not over. Something was still wrong. I told the family I would be back the next morning to minister further.

That night the boy became sick again, both physically and mentally. But instead of calling us like we had asked them to do, they called a nearby doctor who filled him up with dope again. The next morning when we arrived, we found the boy in the same unconscious condition as we first found him the day before. It's a long story. This case took 32 days of battle.

Though this boy was raised as a Christian in a Central American Mission family, at the age of 15 he began to dabble in witchcraft and Spiritism. He worked at a pop bottling company and came into contact with some fellows who practiced occult sciences. They got him curious and then shared books with him on magic, sorcery, witchcraft and Spiritism that circulate widely throughout Latin America. He got intrigued, then obsessed by the idea. He would stay up at night reading, reading, reading. He began to go to some of those Spiritism centers and witchcraft centers, and then he began to go with those young fellows to the cemeteries to engage spirits. This went on for six or eight months and the boy began to go down morally. He began to drink and smoke and even began to support a woman of ill fame at 15 years of age! He just went to pieces.

He was out with one of his buddies on one of his drunken binges when he discovered they ran out of money. What do you think they did? They assaulted and robbed a man. They beat him so badly they thought they had killed him. So, what did they do? They got the body and threw it into a cave, disposed of it.

When the boy went home that night, the house was empty. The family had gone to Guatemala City because his old grandmother had broken her hip. In one of the books he had read he remembered something about a covenant with Satan by which you can receive Satan's favor, promising that Satan will give you whatever you want, whatever you need, whatever you ask.

So, the boy searched for the book and found the covenant with Satan on the last page. It is the strongest covenant any human being can make. He got the book and went out to the pasture.

In the darkness at midnight, he invoked Satan. Whether in body or in vision, I don't know, but Satan appeared to him. This boy entered into a covenant relationship with Satan. He turned himself over to Satan in spirit, soul, and body, and threw himself on him.

Satan promised he would dissolve the body of the beaten and robbed man or make the man's body disappear. He would dissolve the body. He told him he would help him, favor him, and make him rich and famous—as long as this boy served him. But if ever this boy turned his back on Satan, Satan would kill him and all his family. It was a covenant to death.

Things went right for a few months, but he was distressed with the conflict between his Christian upbringing and this new thing that had come into his life. He went to see the movie, Spiritism, in Guatemala. That was the day the conflict came to a head.

One Sunday he decided to go to church, for the first time in years. The next Wednesday he took his bible and tried to memorize John 3:16. In that moment he completely went out of his mind. Crazy. Suddenly. Just like that. What had happened? He had turned his back on Satan by going to church and reading the bible. Satan took revenge, determined to kill him.

That was a Wednesday. His parents called four different doctors in town to take care of him. They filled him with dope and intravenous feedings. They tried their best to bring him out of it. Finally, they said they couldn't do anything more for him and recommended the family take him to Guatemala City and put him under expert care in an insane asylum.

We saw him on Tuesday. We began to deal with this case knowing nothing of this covenant. We literally had no idea. We would cast the devil out and the next day he would be back. He had a right to be there! That boy was his property. He belonged to him. This had me completely baffled; we had already handled a thousand cases, but this was something new. We just didn't know what to do. By Saturday the boy was apparently well so we told his mother it would be all right for him to go back home.

They went back home and decided to have a Thanksgiving service at their home for their son's deliverance and healing that Saturday night. They invited the whole town, including the three pastors of the three churches there. They called and asked me to come up to preach.

During the service, the boy got up and gave his testimony. After he sat down for about five minutes, he turned to me and said, "Norman, I'm feeling awful. I don't know what's happening to me. I have to leave. I feel like I'm going to faint." I felt he was just weary and weak from the terrible strain on him, so I told him to go relieve himself at the outside outhouse. When he went out, he fell flat on his face—fainted. We discovered the boy was already possessed of the devil—again!

You know that brought confusion into that crowd. He had just testified and there he was just as bad as ever! The devil is tricky. He had stopped manifesting himself in this boy for a few days in order to create confusion in the minds of these people who really didn't believe in the power of God.

We continued the battle. It wasn't until 15 days after we began to handle the case that the boy broke down and told us about his covenant with Satan. One night as we were praying and reciting Scripture, the Lord revealed to me the word "covenant". It came straight from heaven. I turned to the boy and said, "Harold? Have you made a covenant with Satan?" He turned pale and began to tremble. When he began to say, "Yes" he fell back, and Satan screamed out of him, "I'm L-A-A-TE!" Just like that.

What had happened? The devil had been out of him. If he hadn't been out of him at the time, I'm sure the boy never would have been able to muster enough courage to confess. When the boy said yes, the enemy entered in and began to speak.

Led of the Holy Spirit, I said, "Satan, right now I bind you and I shut you up in this boy. You will not come out of this body until the Spirit of God leads me!"

I had never done that before. It was something completely different for me. I had Satan bound in that body for ten days. This was the most marvelous experience I've had in my ministry. Ten days. It was a battle because physically, financially, in every way we suffered.

It was during those 10 days we discovered the depths of Satan's power and Satan's work. We actually went behind the veil and saw how Satan operates. During those ten days, that devil revealed who he was. "I am the Prince of Guatemala and surrounding territory. I'm Satan. I'm the overlord of this whole area of the world!" You see, when the boy made the covenant, he made it with the powers that were over that whole area—a principality.

During those ten days we made him confess everything in the name of Jesus. But Satan used every trick of the trade. One day he used Scripture. Oh, he knew the Scriptures inside and out! He would say, "In that day you will say, Lord, Lord, in thy name I cast out devils and the Lord would say, "I never knew you!" The prince said, "That's what's going to happen to you!" That old devil looked me square in my face when he said that.

I said, "Satan, you are the accuser of the brethren." And then he used that passage in Jude: "Even Michael the Archangel dare not bring an accusation against Satan." And added, "Who are you?! Do you think you're better than Michael?"

The next day he changed his tactics saying, "I'm going to test you. I'm going to prove to you that you are going to obey me! Right now, this boy is going to get dressed and go out in the street and commit a crime! He's going to go out, get drunk, and paint the town red. You're going to try to stop him because he's under your care! If you try to stop him, you are actually obeying me because that is what I'm telling you to do!" Do you know what that boy did? He got up, got dressed, and headed towards the door. Naturally the temptation for me was to try to stop him, because if he did something terrible, I would be the one to blame. I would be the guilty party because he was my responsibility. Do you know I didn't move an inch? I stayed there and resisted the devil, saying, "Satan, you are just wasting your time."

When the boy got to the door, he suddenly dropped to the floor. Fell flat on his face. The next day the devil used another technique. "If you will just stop casting out devils, oh, I will make you rich. I will fill this room with gold. I'm not telling you to stop preaching the gospel. Go on and preach, that doesn't create too much havoc in my kingdom. That doesn't bother me. Stop casting out devils and you will gain my favor." It went on like that starting on a Wednesday, then Thursday, Friday, and Saturday he used all these tricks.

By Sunday this old demon was desperate. He no longer threatened; he no longer offered anything. He began to beg! He said, "P-L-E-A-S-E get me out of here, I'm in torment! Now I know what the pit will be. I've never been bound for such a long time in one place. My liberty has been taken away." A number of our pastors were witnesses to this begging. I knew the story was going to be so fantastic that no one would believe it. Satan was bound for ten days! He was sick. He begged and pleaded.

Nine of us went down to the ocean on Wednesday for a three-day retreat to prepare the boy for his final deliverance. We knew it was going to be a battle to death. Satan wasn't going to let that boy go easily; wasn't going to let his prey go. We went with a determination to fast and pray for three days. We didn't take a bit of food.

Thursday morning when we got up, oh, we were all hungry and sick. We all had gnawing pain in our stomachs. We thought maybe it was because we had fasted so often. We asked the lady of the house to prepare some rice and eggs, and we ate.

No sooner had we eaten than that boy sat up and the devil began to laugh hysterically saying, "See what I did? I made you all eat! Here you came with the determination of fasting three days and you couldn't even stand 24 hours!" He got the biggest kick out of it. He said, "I commanded my spirits to attack you, create hunger, and create pain and nausea so you would eat!"

Every day we had maybe two times to talk to this demon because we couldn't pray with the boy—he would immediately go unconscious! The evil spirit would not stand for prayer in the Holy Spirit. This boy tried to study the Scriptures but as soon as he would open the Bible it would go blank on him. Satan would blind him to God's Word.

For example, one day we were sitting at the table eating and some of the young people from Guatemala City Church were there. Suddenly one of the boys turned to me and said, "Norman, could somebody who's made a covenant with Satan be forgiven?" I had never told anybody about this case or that the boy had made a covenant with Satan. Yet, this boy suddenly came up with that question out of the blue!

I looked at poor Haroldo and he was just ready to collapse as though he had been hit over the head with a ball bat. We discovered that little young fellow, 14 years of age, needed deliverance too. The devil was busy. Three times in two days, three different teenage boys asked the same question to torment Haroldo and put in his mind that he had no forgiveness from God. I'm just giving you tidbits.

We were at the ocean and discovered that since the spirit was the Prince of Guatemala other demons would come to him to get their orders. There was constant demon activity around this boy.

Sometimes other demons would manifest and talk through him. For example, one demon came, and I said, "Where did you come from?" And he said, "I come from Tapachula, Mexico."

I asked, "Who sent you?" "Witchdoctors sent me." "Why did they send you?" He began to inform us the witchdoctors there banded together working against us. We were about 200—300 miles away. These Centers have intercommunication through demons. There is a systematic, controlling network. They knew where we were and what we were doing. When the evil spirit in this boy got really desperate, he actually began to offer to turn against his kingdom saying, "If you let me out, I will destroy three of my greatest witchcraft centers in Guatemala. I thought, "If he offers, it must be possible." I didn't take him up on his offer, but I did command him to do a lot of things. Since then do you know what we discovered?

When dealing with cases of demon possession that are caused by witchcraft and Spiritism, we can close and destroy those gates of hell centers that bring people into bondage. Scores of witchcraft centers and Spiritist centers in Guatemala have been shuttered. We have known of witchdoctors and Spiritist mediums who have actually died under the wrath of God a few days after someone had been delivered, who had been brought into bondage by their operation. We've learned we can take those centers, no longer just delivering a person and leaving that center open so it can cause more havoc among the people of God. We can take authority over them. We have more power than we realize.

In Guatemala the evil spirits are "centered." They are divided into different centers from where their higher powers plan strategies and give orders. We can take authority and command those evil spirits to not only depart, but also command them to go back and tell that witchdoctor, or medium, or sorcerer, or power that he can no longer operate because the Lord Jesus Christ is victor. That's it. The center closes.

Friday, we returned to Guatemala City after spending three days at the ocean, and after that we fasted, prayed, and studied about spiritual warfare in the Book of Joshua. Every so often that demon we were dealing with became really active. He threatened that if we went back to Huehuetenango, the city where this boy lived, that he would make our plane crash or our car crash. He was going to prevent our return. He told us that three of the most powerful witchdoctors in Guatemala were headed towards Huehuetenango to stop us from coming. They were going there to begin work 24 hours a day to hinder the deliverance of this boy.

We found out they went there. They went Friday. We went Saturday. We had no trouble because "the angel of the Lord encamps round about them that fear Him (Psalm 34:7). We determined that the boy's family would know nothing of this. We only told his mother as much as was necessary.

Because the covenant was mutual, I said to the boy, "Saturday night we will go out to the pasture where you made this covenant. I said to Satan, "The boy broke his part in this when he entered into a covenant relationship with me based upon Matthew 18:19. Satan, you have to break your part of the covenant!"

At 4:00 o'clock the boy said, "I'm tired and I'm awfully cold. I'm going to go lie down for a little while" Now we were about 9000 feet above sea level; it's cold there. When he lay down, his mother rushed in with a cover. Harold was no longer conscious, so it was Satan who was talking, "I can't stand it another moment! Right here and now I break the covenant I entered into with this boy!" When the Prince of Guatemala broke the covenant, he came rushing out in a legion, coming out by groups, screaming their names and departing! This boy had demons from his childhood. You know how that happened? His great grandmother was a witch in a nearby town! When she died a few months after this boy was born, the demons that were in her entered the boy. Demons seek another body and usually seek another body in the same family.

We've had another case where a boy raised up in our church, whose father had been an elder in our church in Guatemala City and died of cancer of the kidney. When this boy came back to the church ten years later, a demon of kidney cancer manifested himself. I commanded the demon to tell me when he had entered. He said, "When the boy's father died, I passed from the father into him." Sometimes I think a lot of inherited disease comes that way.

So Haroldo had demons of all kinds. I couldn't even count. They just came out by groups. I thought that was the end of the battle. Do you know what happened after? This is something you might not understand and might not accept. When that boy was finally delivered that day, another voice spoke saying, "I'm the angel of David, sent of the Lord." Well, I had been deceived before by demons that call themselves angels. The

Bible says to believe not the spirits. Try the spirits. Put them to the test.

I said, "Spirit, I command you in the name of Jesus Christ to confess Jesus Christ came in the flesh." The spirit said, "Yes." Well, I don't stop very long because one spirit answered "Yes" but was in fact a demon. I once dealt with a demon who said he was the Archangel Michael! I was nearly convinced but something told me to go a little further. I asked, "What did Jesus come for?" "Oh, he came to give a good example. You know, modernistic preaching. He came to teach. He came to heal." I said, "Now spirit, I command you to tell me what it says in 1 John 3:8: "For this purpose the Son of God was manifested, that he might ... what?" He wouldn't say it. He wouldn't say it because the devil won't confess that Jesus came to destroy the works of the devil!

I thought that was the end. The next day we went around visiting. A lot of Catholic people wanted to know about this case of deliverance, about healing. At about noon, the boy said, "I'm tired. I'm going home." I said, "Go on. When I finish rounds, I'll be back."

When I got there, we were sitting around the table having some coffee with bread. As I was sitting there, his mother came in in a panic and said, "Haroldo needs you!" So, I went into his room where he was sleeping. Haroldo said, "I'm dying Norman. I feel death creeping up my leg." I said, "Move your leg." He couldn't; he was paralyzed. You know what I thought? This boy has been poisoned. We had been to different Catholic homes and they'd given us coffee and pop, and I thought somehow these witchdoctors have gotten poison. I got him over my knee and began to repeat Scripture about poison and how it shall not harm you. Suddenly I said, "Spirit I command you to tell me your name!" He said, "I am Death."

You know what had happened? Those three major witchdoctors of Guatemala were still working! They hadn't given up. They had been working from Friday to Sunday. Satan had already departed and had gone back to report what had happened, but the witchdoctors had agreed that at 4:00 Sunday afternoon they were going to cast the strongest spell on that boy that can ever be cast on a human being: a spell of instantaneous death. The boy was done.

Well, when I knew it was Death, I got ahold of that body and we began to actually wrestle him. We began to fly through that room, knocking over chairs and tables. I had to cry out, "Lord, give me strength!" It was the most terrible battle I've ever had—15 minutes. I wouldn't let that body die. I said, "Satan you are not going to rob God of this trophy of grace and power."

After 15 minutes, I was able to subdue him, and he began to throw up blood coming from his heart. I was troubled because I thought the previous day it had all ended.

As soon as this boy was delivered an angel spoke saying, "I am angel Gabriel." I replied, "Why did this happen? I mean, I thought this was ended and that the angels were taking care of it. He said, "The Lord has called us to step aside so that you can receive training. This is your spiritual

DIVERSE DELIVERANCE CASES

training. The Lord is preparing you." The angel said, "The spell the three witchdoctors released on this boy goes back on their heads! They die now!" And it happened under the wrath of God. Why? Because the Bible says, "What you sow you shall reap."

The boy was delivered of death itself, finally and completely. Today this boy is beginning to serve the Lord. In a recent letter, he told us he had preached his first sermon in a little church and three souls had been saved. He's won some of his buddies at work too. The Lord is training and raising him up little by little. We can expect great things from him. These are the young people we should be praying for and trying to help that the Lord might use them mightily in these last days.

The battle in Guatemala has been rough but the power of God is greater. "Greater is He that is in you than he that is in the world" (1 John 4:4).

In a related case, one of the greatest centers in Guatemala City had a witchdoctor who was a naturalist. Thousands of people came to see him. On certain consultation days he would have scores of cars—rich people—coming to find favor from him.

There was a man who attended our church in Guatemala City who was a graduate of the Bible Institute. He entered the ministry, but something happened in his life and he began to attend the Center of Spiritism. He became secretary of that center. A pastor! A man trained and ordained for the ministry! He stopped going to church but one of his sons began coming to our church. Today he is our best friend and through this boy we were able to win back the whole family. When we came in contact with the family, his father stopped going to the center! Two years later the man died the most horrible death, dying in agony; it was the most terrible thing. He died in agony of cancer, which ate up the whole inside of him.

When I was dealing with the covenant case about Haroldo and I was dealing with the prince, I commanded him to tell me how that man had died. I didn't know the details at the time. The demon told me the story. He said, "When that man left the center to go back to the Christian church, the witchdoctor cast a spell on him to kill him because he knew too much." I asked his family if it was true, he had gone to the Spiritist center and his wife told the whole story. Actually, when I heard the full story, that center was one of the ones I commanded to be destroyed. One day soon after, I drove by the center on a day they used to have those big crowds coming and there wasn't a soul around. It had been destroyed.

We have more power than we realize. We have not really risen up to claim our rights in the Lord Jesus Christ. We have not taken all the authority that Christ has given us as sons of God over all the kingdom of Satan. I believe God is going to permit us to claim our spiritual inheritance so that when Satan attacks, we will not only stand, cross our arms, grit our teeth, and tough it out, but rather rise up and take the offensive against him! God is raising an army of mighty, valiant men and women anointed of the Spirit to storm the very gates of hell!

UNIVERSITY PRESIDENT, DR. NICK

The deliverance of Dr. Nick provides a spiritual template for anyone who genuinely desires to work in Christian exorcism—more often referred to as deliverance ministry in Christian circles. First, the minister must be a believing Christian, and second, the person seeking deliverance must be, or become, a believer in Jesus Christ as personal Savior. It would be dangerous for any pretender or unbeliever to attempt such a deliverance, as seen in the biblical example of the *"seven sons of Sceva"* (See Acts 19:13-16).

Rev. Rodney G. Lensch, a Lutheran minister asked me to accompany him for ministry to an out-of-state friend whose line of work required frequent airline travel. His problem was terror of heights and of flying that tormented him. He also had arthritis and the propensity to inflict pain upon his wife during intimate relations—a form of sadism.

After an evening of acquaintance, there were four hours of interviewing the husband the next morning. There was a separate, lesser session with his wife, during which the man's symptoms and our diagnoses would be ascertained and confirmed. I took notes for reference during later prayer time. Discerning of spirits occurs primarily during the interview, and less during the heat of combat. This approach is especially helpful during private ministry sessions when sufficient time can be devoted to get to the specific details of the issues.

The gentleman candidate was president of an engineering college at a major university. He was a moderate, believing Christian who attended a mainline, denominational church.

The second evening was action time. He was asked to sit in a straight back chair in the center of the room. This is preferred so that the minister can have full access to the person to be delivered. My associate was seated fifteen feet away to observe, while I stood facing the man, giving him final instructions.

As usual in a private setting, I first explained what might be expected in a supernatural clash of warring adversaries. There can be physical violence on the part of demons resisting expulsion and things can get noisy. In essence, I explained the direction we were going to take and the prayers that both of us would be praying in agreement. I explained how I would lead the candidate in the prayer, phrase by phrase, which he would repeat aloud. The prayer would cover the legal bases that would undermine the demons' ability to seriously resist. It also would ensure that all concerned would understand the power of agreement when praying in one accord.

Laying the groundwork prevents delays and disruptions in the spiritual flow, once engaged in battle. All in attendance must agree on the biblical basis for the encounter, the process, and in the need to rely upon the Holy Spirit to lend his power to the minister's commanding words: We stand on Jesus's words in Mark 16:15-20 as our authority. The blood of Jesus is invoked. Jesus' resurrection proves God accepted Jesus' sacrifice for our sins—the debt paid in full. It is on this basis that Satan no longer has the right or power to withstand our command to depart.

The confessing Christian, therefore, must be released from Satan's bondage and torments. In preparation it was my practice to pray with fasting to demonstrate my dependence upon the Lord, and to emphasize my strong desire and willingness to minister as He would lead.

Once all this was fully settled, it was time to initiate action, first by thanking the Lord in verbal prayer of agreement for this wonderful privilege. Our commands would not need to be loud, because the demons would already have heard our discussion, explanation, and the basis for exercising the authority Jesus delegated to us. They knew it was the truth and were fully aware that we also knew it. Now it was only a matter of forcing the issue.

I laid my right hand on Dr. Nick's forehead to impart the substance of spirit. We prayed a prayer of command and confession, standing on the biblical principle, "...one would chase a thousand, and two put ten thousand to flight..." (Deuteronomy 32:30) and, "Two are better than one; because they have a good reward for their labour" (Ecclesiastes 4:9).

I instructed him to repeat after me, breaking the prayer into small phrases like this:

Lord Jesus Christ, I do believe that you died on the Cross to save me from my sins;

You descended into hell and preached to the captives,

You arose on the third day, victorious over death, hell, and the grave,

And made an open show of Satan's defeat.

That you ascended from the grave to the right hand of the Father, where you now intercede on my behalf.

I acknowledge and repent of all my sins, known and unknown.

Please forgive me.

I forgive all others who have ever hurt, harmed, or said bad things to me or about me,

Just as fully as I ask you to forgive me,

I ask you to deliver me now from these tormenting demons, for which I will ever be grateful and give praise to your name. Amen."

Still leading him in prayer, "Now, Satan I come against you in the name of the Lord Jesus Christ,

Applying His Blood, on the authority of the Word of God, in the anointing of the Holy Spirit.

It is time to pack your bags and prepare to depart.

You no longer have any power or authority over me.

I command you to come up and depart from my soul and body which are the property of the Lord Jesus Christ, who paid for them by his precious Blood.

I continued to lead Dr. Nick in addressing specific demons as follows:

I address you, Fear of Heights and Fear of Flying in aircraft, come out in Jesus' name!

Arthritis, I bind you from manifesting; get out now!

You spirit of Sadistic Sex, release your hold and get out of this house (referring to his human body).

All you tormenters, and you supportive spirits of a kindred nature, get out of me now.

At this point I instructed Dr. Nick to cease all talking as Reverend Lensch and I released the power of the Holy Spirit by speaking in tongues in accordance with Mark 16:17, Acts 2:4 and Acts 19:6.

In deliverance ministry, it is important to instruct the candidate to stop talking after they have prayed. Their breathing canal and vocal cords must be left open and unused, thus leaving room for the demons to be expelled more easily through that passageway.

Within moments of giving the command, the fingers on both of Dr. Nick's hands went stiff and straight—very rigid—turning white, cold, and clammy. Interestingly, these are the same manifestations that can occur when fighting against spirits of masturbation and nicotine—as each of them requires the use of one's fingers.

I put my hands on both of his - palms against palms - firmly interlocking my fingers with his while continuing the battle. The chair began to rock to and fro, as our tightly engaged arms carried opposing powers in battle. Our superior power in Christ prevented the demons from traveling forward to me. Within 30 minutes they expired!

The act of interlocking my fingers with Nick's was in no way an invitation to a demon to transfer from him into me—that would be foolish, and result in calamity, for spirits would indeed transfer! On the contrary, it was the most direct way to impart the force of the Holy Spirit against the evil spirits operating in Dr. Nick's hands and fingers, applying pressure to precisely where they were manifesting.

Exerting Holy Spirit power and authority through direct contact on the specific location of demonic activity in the body helps to overcome them. This is where the natural engages the supernatural. Wonderfully, the effort paid off and the mission was accomplished in full measure. It is important to note that within the bounds of decency, I have learned to place my hands exactly where the demon is (just as a surgeon probes the afflicted part of the body), but always with permission of the candidate.

At mid-point in the process, I called to my colleague to come and lay hands on the center of the back of his friend, in support of the prayer effort. Due to his minimal deliverance experience, Reverend Lensch tentatively complied. Altogether, everything worked as it should, fire being imparted from the back and the front by the two of us working in harmony. Dr. Nick was the grateful beneficiary. The demons were gone.

Enroute to home afterward, Reverend Lensch exclaimed, "Man! David, you really have to be *called* to do that kind of ministry!" I received his message in humility, knowing it is the Lord who does the heavy lifting. That said, it is also true that Jesus' command was to "them that believe" (Mark 16: 17). Deliverance ministry is not limited to a gifted few. It is for every true believer. Like muscles, spiritual gifts grow stronger and more defined with use. Deliverance work should be done by every Christian. Suppose, for example, that 600 million Christians were to cast out one demon per year. In five years, the dent in Satan's kingdom would be enormous—he would have **30 billion** fewer demon warriors infiltrating

Christians! It is only a matter of believing and acting on our God-given mandate! What is the Church waiting for?

Soon enough, Dr. Nick wrote a thank you letter for the miraculous intervention on behalf of his family and himself. Such acknowledgment makes it all the more rewarding, though not necessary ... and in truth, is often not received.

You should not expect acclaim, human reward, money, or popularity in this work; usually it is quite the opposite, being especially unpopular among churches whose theology won't allow the Lord's "disruptive work" to be done in their parish. Further contact from the party who has received the benevolence is unlikely. Most do not want to rehearse the pain of their demonic plight and it's an unfortunate stigma emanating from the Church at large. That *stigma* is a reproach upon the Church leadership. Nevertheless, we as individuals, must do what Jesus commanded and personally demonstrated. See Mark 9:17-29 to learn what may occur.

Deliverance ministry—helping others in Jesus' name—is costly. Part of the price is that of maintaining a high level of devotion and holiness before the Lord, lest one become disqualified from privileged fellowship of the angelic and Holy Spirit empowering to dispense such a grace.

While these facts are straightforward enough to understand, a few points are important enough to emphasize with supporting scriptures:

"...thou hast magnified thy word above all thy name" (Psalm 138:2b).

"Is not my word like as a fire? Saith the Lord; and like a hammer that breaketh the rock in pieces?" (Jeremiah 23:29)

"Not by might, nor by power, but by my spirit saith the Lord of hosts." (Zechariah 4:6b)

"But truly I am full of power by the spirit of the Lord..." (Micah 3:8)

"But if I cast out devils [evil spirits - demons] by the Spirit of God, then the kingdom of God is come upon you." (Matthew 12:28)

Needing emphasis are "word" and "Spirit." The words of God are as a hammer and the Spirit of God is manifested as fire and power (*firepower*). Both fire and power are required to force supernatural agents to yield and flee. Notice especially that the highest possible authority is the Word, which is magnified even above the all-powerful name of the Lord. This means if we had to choose only one weapon against the devil, it should be the Word of God. The demon would have to yield his position and flee based upon the commanding Word alone.

The Holy Spirit always acts in concert with the Word, for Jesus Himself is the Word (See John 1:1). Thus, invoking the Word is equivalent to invoking Jesus. Oftentimes, using faith on the offensive, the mere quoting of pertinent Scriptures will cause the demon to depart. Demons know they must yield to the Word, which is the highest authority possible. Ultimately, they know they will bow before the name of Jesus and be made to confess that He is the only true Lord (See Philippians 2:10-11).

While fire consumes chaff, the evil rock may require numerous blows of the hammer to be broken into pieces. If rock refers to a cluster of demons, multiple blows of the hammer will cause the unlinking of demons from one another. Separately each is easily removed. Parenthetically, kidney stones are removed in the same way—fragmented to bits first, then expelled. It has been my dubious privilege to savor that painful procedure several times, doubtless the Lord's doing, to emphasize the point for your benefit!

Even after the demonic rock has been broken and the fragments evicted, further instruction is found in Matthew 12:43-45: "When the unclean spirit [fragment] is gone out of a man, he walketh through dry places seeking rest and findeth none. Then he saith, I will return into my house from whence I came out; and when he is come, he findeth it empty, swept, and garnished. Then goeth he, and taketh with himself seven other spirits more wicked than himself, and they enter in and dwell there: and the state of that man is worse than the first …". This warning tells us the war has not ended when a single battle has been won. The deliverance minister, as well as the person delivered, are now required to live a holy life, filled with the Spirit of God.

The problem Jesus presents is that the house was left empty. The Holy Spirit had not been invited to fill the vacancy. Qualified realtors know the danger of leaving a house vacant. An empty house is not only subject to vandalism, but also to unauthorized squatters—in this case, squatter spirits.

Notice the original doorkeeper spirit was not as wicked as the other seven demons that followed him back into the house. The end result was much worse than before. The mild-mannered doorkeeper spirit returns with a whole new gang of wicked despots who must be wrestled out the door.

Carrying it one step further, our thoughts, motives, imaginations, meditations, and actions should become infused with the words, the name, and the character of the Lord. "If we live in the Spirit, let us also walk in the Spirit" (Galatians 5:25). This is the original perfect standard before sin entered.

Obviously, there is a lot of work to be done along the way to meet the standard. It will mostly be accomplished by the Lord, but with our cooperation. Therefore, let us proceed to destroy the works of the devil as Jesus commanded.

3

AUTHOR'S BIOGRAPHY

Possibly you have been as impressed as I was at the revelation inherent in Patty's deliverance. None other of this magnitude has been published to my knowledge. The type, depth, and clarity of Satan's network was never previously exposed so glaringly. Other accounts have provided glimpses, overviews from Scripture, and specific effects of deliverance upon individuals. Among them is the book written by Jesse Penn-Lewis in 1912, War On The Saints.

It is the most complete and complex revealing of the deceptive manner in which one may be snared by Satan's workings, but primarily within an individual's mind, emotions, and body. It is magnificent and unparalleled. My reading of it was mentally tedious in learning how to apply its detailed teaching to obtain personal relief, but it was foundational, informational, and helpful indeed. Yet, a few revelation details of the devil's worldwide network were to wait 53 years until Patty's deliverance.

Through it several missing details became known, both in the direct, simple language and demonstrations of demons themselves, and of us ministers battling them. Another report that undergirds the narrative about Patty is the personal work and testimony of Missionary Norman Parish, who destroyed a demonic network in Guatemala, Central America, which extended into neighboring countries. His experience is detailed in Chapter One, which further exposes the networks of Satan. It enlarges upon the territory dimension observed through Patty's deliverance.

Also, the importance of several books generally on this subject is not to be minimized. Their combined modern-day content confirms the ongoing deliverance ministry of Jesus and his true followers of our day. Though the Lord's call was never modified from its requirement of believers, its practice has long been neglected to the detriment of the church at large.

In reading the various books I have benefited by receiving physical and spiritual deliverance, conducting teaching seminars, and performing numerous such miracles in others. No such reading or event was so enlightening, however, as my direct participation in Patty's multiple deliverances seven years apart. Indeed, without them this book could not have been written because her deliverances are its core.

Hopefully, this exposé of Satan's network and workings will enlighten ordinary believers to a fuller understanding of their own spiritual power and encourage them to attack their spiritual enemies in a similar way. If that is achieved, the Twenty First Century could yet become the most prolific ever in destroying the works of the devil. The sleeping giant of uninformed Christians is being awakened. When Jesus proclaimed, "Greater things than these shall they do in my name" (John 14:12), he seems to have meant greater in quantity if not in type. Let us proceed in doing those works.

UPDATE ON PATTY

The remarkable story of Patty would not be complete without revealing how her post-deliverance life has unfolded. My good fortune has been to re-establish fellowship with her during the final stage of this writing. Our conversations are now regular, even during her international travels. After her deliverance from the evil powers she successfully completed her career as mobile and hospital nurse, which was 61 years of dedicated service. She retired in 2016 at age 82. Both during and after her career she has remained an active member of the same church where she had been thoroughly trained in Bible Study and in foreign missions.

To give you a sense of how our spiritual relationship had developed, I have printed my letter to her, handwritten after we first became re-acquainted by telephone in 2017. It somewhat shows how profoundly and deeply our mutual deliverance experiences melded our spirits. Content of this letter, together with the deliverance report, may reignite your enthusiasm to learn more of this subject, the realization of which could change the course of your life for the better, as it did for Patty and for my family.

My Dear Patty –

How exciting and marvelous to talk to you again after half a century! Most of your British accent has "passed away" – yet your spirit has not waned. You are still self-effacing, not realizing how important and far-reaching your life has been.

My dear, your deliverance was the most wondrous experience of my Christian life. What happened there changed the whole course of my life. Everything that has been ministered through Nancy and me pivoted on your deliverance and testimony. Effectively, your life and service to the Lord has reached around the world. It helped launch me into both direct deliverance ministry and into serving 600 missionaries and ministries worldwide for 42 years.

Several years ago, I gave a copy of your testimony to a missionary in Tanzania, Africa. She and her husband have taught startling lessons out of it to their ministry students. Now it is featured in our new book: "War of the World, Flesh, and the Devil. It is my firm belief that your testimony will impact millions. Moreover, your testimony is also my testimony. For I, too, was prayed for 24 hours after Derek Prince prayed for you. Your experience was more dramatic, but mine was also extensive over time. You and I were blended in spirit upon first meeting, and over the next several years at Faith Tabernacle. I was so impressed when you revealed your bravery and courage in standing at the pulpit before a large congregation to give intimate testimony. Not many would do that to the extent you did.

Never has a month passed in the last 50 years that I haven't thought of you. I first wrote the report of your testimony in a third-floor attic in 1972. It has been part of my spiritual fabric ever since. Editor of Christian Life Magazine – Bob Walker – wanted to publish it then, but I declined. Now, however, as the spiritual days have darkened, it is the right time.

Patty, I never think of you without remembering the gentle softness of your voice – modulated by the Holy Spirit – to bring us a spiritual message from among the congregation. It stood out from others – sweet, mellow, feminine, and appropriate. Derek Prince then confirmed its application to us. I observed it all from the tape recorder booth beside the stage.

Suddenly, I realize how fleeting a single human life is – 70 to 80 years or so. Please realize that your life shall yet have great godly impact, as it already has. In 1966 at Faith Tabernacle, Derek and Lydia Prince answered a question I had put to them. It was about fervent prayer as relates to its volume or loudness. Derek answered: "It is often the quietest of men who are the most fervent." That satisfied me. You likewise are quiet and fervent in faith. The more commonplace good things you and we have done the past 50 years may pale in comparison to the revelation in your deliverance testimony. As Mordecai the Jew said to Queen Esther, "… who knoweth whether thou art come to the kingdom for such a time as this?" (Esther 4:14)

Publication of your story could not be timelier. It should encourage Jews and Christians, as well as enlighten unbelievers everywhere, not just in Israel. May it be so. Dear Patty, I know about many of the abrasions and loneliness of your life, and you understand they redound to the glory of God. Apostle Paul called them, "…our light affliction which is but for a moment" (2 Corinthians 4:17). We both know some of that and shall forever praise the Lord together.

It is uncertain whether we shall meet again on earth. But it is certain we shall meet again. Rejoice with me at the soon prospect of rejoining all our friends and family of faith in the better place. My personal family has agreed to meet in the Armenian Quarter.

Come see us! Many blessings upon you. Amen.

Love in Christ,
David Keklikian

HARD THINGS OF GOD

Writing appropriate portions of my biography may reveal a path the Lord often arranges to develop qualified servants. Tests and trials are His means of producing right character. An analogy may be seen in the defined hardness that has to be melded into the most critical parts of an aircraft. While working at Douglas Aircraft Company as Precision Parts Inspector, careful inspection of certain parts was necessary to verify they passed the Rockwell Hardness Test. An inspection certified that they would not fail under extraordinary pressures of use. As it is in the natural, so it is in the spiritual realm, where the Lord is both Manufacturer and Inspector.

He, too, requires the passing of hardness tests. Spiritual warriors must be able to withstand extraordinary spiritual pressures. Tests come almost as a curriculum of crises, isolations, betrayals, and adversities on various fronts. They include financial uncertainties, treacheries by family and friends, abandonments, disillusionment, and anxieties that approach the point of despair.

Several examples in Scripture are Saul of Tarsus on the road to Damascus being struck blind from heaven by Jesus Himself, chosen to suffer as no other man; Joseph betrayed and sold into slavery by his brothers; David being falsely accused, targeted for death, and relentlessly pursued by King Saul and his troops. Abraham was required to slay his only son; Jesus was betrayed by disciple Judas Iscariot; thrice denied by his close friend, Peter, at the worst possible moment. There are more such tests, which most Christians have read in Scripture that prove the point. The ultimate *hardness test* is obedience to the command of Christ to forgive friends and enemies who painfully damage us.

Though forgiveness is required, we are not abandoned to it alone. Just as with agents of darkness, God likewise has provided helpers. The primary source of information on both is the Holy Bible. Reference to other biblical books also may be researched. Evangelist Billy Graham wrote one titled, *Angels: God's Secret Agents*, which explains their work of helping believers in distress. Our book has similarities, but its thrust is more the deliverance from the tormenting works of dark angels and demons, with the help of holy angels and the

Spirit of the Lord. More titles and resources are listed in the back of this book.

Thus, we see from our beginnings that both good and evil forces have been engaged in combat over human loyalties. Their presence has not been episodic but continuous from the first man. A few occasions of their battles - such as in Patty's deliverance and Norman Parish's warfare - are extraordinarily revealing and necessary for us to witness. Without them we could only try to believe that such biblical accounts were true by faith alone, without seeing a shred of evidence. They show us that Christians should not be mere bystanders but rather be proactively engaged with other brethren in this War of the World, Flesh, and the Devil. I emphasize being proactive because nearly all the reports given in public media, Christian and Secular, are *after the fact* of Satan's damaging onslaughts. Open displays of our preemptive, victorious engagements must be vastly increased. This is the meaning of proactive – acting in advance to prevent the carnage.

These studies are intended to give impetus for active participation by ordinary folks, and to provide actionable knowledge of how we are to engage and defeat the enemy. Our arsenal of weapons for spiritual warfare has proved to be potently effective in achieving personal victory against intractable strongholds. Primary among them are appropriate application of the Blood of Jesus, the Word of God, praying of warfare prayers, and giving clear verbal commands in the authority Jesus gave us. Together these defeat the adversary.

These several accounts show exactly how you and I must use them to be successful. There are a few other weapons shown in Ephesians 6, but without the atomic power of these four there can be no certain victory.

At stake are exceedingly great spoils to the Victor, supreme among which are human loyalty, eternal worship, glory and praise to God, brought about through our allegiance to Him now and forever. For the vanquished, however, quite the opposite "reward" awaits. Those who align with the rebellion shall forever be imprisoned where no reprieve, abatement, parole, or escape shall ever be possible. Thanks be to God.

As to the effectiveness of two general styles of ministry among the many, we see that in very large gatherings there typically are a few public spectacles of miraculous happenings. The late evangelist, Oral Roberts, claimed less than three percent of those he prayed for received a miracle. That low percent, however, is quite obviously of immeasurable significance to those who received. Also, a high-profile minister is typically elevated and glorified among the greater number in attendance and may receive considerable funds out of large collections of money.

Such a presiding pastor/evangelist is subjected to less personal pressure by reason of the multitude of believers exercising faith on his behalf. In this way the power of the enemy is somewhat dissipated. The disadvantage, however, is that a majority of needy believers do not receive what they had hoped and prayed for. This situation prevails in most large congregations of believers everywhere.

In comparison, an individual who privately ministers deliverance may rightly expect 100% to receive their miracle. In this venue the minister becomes physically weary, God alone receives all the glory, donations of money to him/her are rare, small, or none, and the daring minister is more likely to die young from the pressures of religious scorn, rejection, poverty, and over-exertion.

In other words, on average the greater the size of the crowd the more diffuse the effectiveness for in depth and enduring ministry to all the needy. What it means in this more private style of ministry, however, is that for the individual-miraculous to become truly widespread, each and every warrior must be a fully engaged participant, not an admiring spectator. I am able to attest to considerable accuracy in the description of the second type of ministry.

In church membership at large, can you think of any who might need deliverance? And, if so, who might be qualified to provide it? The answer to the first question is revealed in the fact that all disciples of Jesus do, and always have lived in a hostile environment amid known and unknown enemies visible and invisible, who variously outnumber them ten to one or more.

If we would honestly strip off the religious masks of pretense, pride and prejudice, occasioned by culturally induced fear of man, we would find that most of us now are generally as Patty was before her deliverance, that is, steeped in the "spirit of the world" [1 Corinthians 2:12] exuding the carnal nature. The mirror exposing it is Philippians 5:19-21, which describes our condition at the moment we realized our need of salvation.

In contrast, verses 22-26 show the great gulf each of us must breach to escape our comparative mediocrity. Such a high plateau cannot be reached by catapulting but must be achieved via a lifetime of personal warfare against the enemy within. The resulting transformation from the one side to the other is to be as observable as night is from day. In view of these scriptures, again we may ask, who besides a Pharisee would dare say he needs no deliverance? Style of ministry is less important than the result obtained, which finally must be obedience to Christ, increasingly revealed in our holy style of life and thought.

OUR ENABLING AND GIFTING

Since we are not left alone to bridge that great gulf, how is it that we are enabled? Again, we turn to the Holy Bible to learn that not everyone has been equally gifted or called. That there are degrees of gifting and anointing by the Holy Spirit is made unmistakably clear: 1 Corinthians 12:4-7 tells us: "Now there are diversities, but the same Spirit. And there are differences of administration, but the same Lord. And there are diversities of operations, but it is the same God which worketh all in all. But the manifestation of the Spirit is given to every man to profit withal."

The next few verses show nine gifts the Lord provides. Further evidence is in James 1:17: "Every good and every perfect gift is from above, and cometh down from the Father...." Clearly, we do not generate our own gifts.

How do we recognize the gift? Some are given more than one. Early in spiritual life one's gifts may not be fully known. Tests are to be applied in order to discover them. A secular example is telecasts of competitions that show differing levels of talent, such as singing voice, physical strength, sports agility, oratory, ability to memorize and spell difficult words, teaching, etc. Few excel, but everyone has a gift that will be revealed by exercise.

So it is in evaluating spiritual gifts – not in competition, but by experimental exercise of them in faith. The secular winner is highly rewarded and made proud. But in the spiritual, the one who fights sufficiently to survive a life of fiery trials and tests is humbled. He knows that both the trials and the gifts come down from God to develop a servant in obedience and humility.

EXAMPLE OF CHANGE

My life was transformed by process in two distinct periods. First was early introduction to primitive Christianity by well-meaning parents faithful in their call, now enjoying their reward in heaven. They had developed most graces and gifts but lacked the knowledge contained in these pages. Their religious conduct in most ways was commendable but was mixed with overbearing demonic influence in the family. Its toxic mix was strenuously rejected, propelling me into unbelief, rebellion, and atheism with its inevitable life style.

Beginning with Patty's deliverance twenty-five years later, however, the transformation began with astronomical speed.

AUTHOR'S BIOGRAPHY

It was my first seeing, hearing, and participating in the unseen reality of supernatural beings. On my part that experience came as a stunning surprise, but from the Lord's point of view it was simply the next step of His curriculum in smoothing the rough edges of a rebel. Here marks the end of the report of Patty's remarkable deliverance. And while it had been a most comprehensive one, there was substantially more to be seen from her within the decade that followed.

After two years of our family's fellowship with Patty under the teaching of Derek Prince, I announced my new work assignment. Church elders Derek Prince, Cliff Claeson, brothers Henry and Gunner Carlson, Rev. DeVore Walterman, and Marcus Lehman prayed, laying on hands, commissioning us for the new ministry and travels. We went to work at Bible Voice Publishers in North Hollywood, California. Leaders George Otis Sr. and Rev. Harald Bredesen were in fellowship with singer Pat Boone, helping to publish his book, A New Song, which relates Pat Boone's then fresh encounter with the Holy Spirit.

TEST OF OBEDIENCE

Seven years after her major exorcism, in 1972 Patty expressed need for further deliverance. Traveling back to Chicago from our California base we interviewed her at length about new and recurrent problems. Near the end she blurted out, "I HATE the Jews!" Whereupon, I instinctively replied, "Jesus is a Jew!" With an audible gasp, she saw the terrible mistake it was to have spoken those words. No one knew better than she that Jesus was both the Chief Jew and her only Deliverer. She covered her face with both hands and sobbed in shame, repenting to the uttermost. I rejoice in tears recalling that tender, blessed moment – much as holy angels rejoice in heaven when one soul repents of sin (Luke 15:10).

The Lord received her tears of honest repentance and sorrow of heart. How wondrous He is! In truth, a tormenting demon had put those words in her mouth, for they, indeed, hate Jesus and other Jews because He destroyed their power by resurrecting from the dead, and will ultimately rule over all nations from Jerusalem, Israel. Not only that, He will cast Satan and his demons into hell. Do you think this could account for animosity between the two kingdoms?

Patty had harbored resentment that developed during the years she worked in a hospital. A spirit of Death had entered her after killing her patient named "Mr. Brown", from which spirit she had been delivered seven years earlier. Resentment, along with Fear, is probably the most common door through which demons enter. Proof that her repentance was accepted is that five demons were then expelled in the name of the Lord.

Pain was another who had returned, hurting her legs as before. This occurred in spite of the outward appearance she was living a model Christian life. But apparent model behavior outwardly had not prevented evil spirits from reentering through the open door of internal resentment. This fact must be learned by all of us. "Man looks on the outward appearance, but the Lord looks upon the heart." So also does Satan to the extent he is able to see.

It was during these seven days of interview and fellowship that we learned of two occasions of deliverance Patty had received in 1960 in Canada, and in 1961 in Chicago. Neither did we know of three others that occurred after that of 1965 reported above. Those were 1968 and 1971 events ministered by missionaries on leave from Kenya, Africa; mutual friends Cas and Lida Knoester. The final occasion was in 1972 with the Knoesters, my wife and myself ministering the expulsion of Witchcraft. This spirit also had re-entered after his defeat in 1965, which I had witnessed.

At least fifteen demons were dealt with during the seven days of our renewed fellowship. What this exemplifies is the teaching of Jesus in Luke 11:24-26, that an evil spirit, once expelled, may return to again enter into the same person ["my house"]. Worse, he would bring in seven others, more wicked than himself. The result quite obviously would be that the original problem would become disastrous by multiplication. This occurs when repentance in heart and mind is not thorough at the occasion of the original expulsion through the mercy and grace of God. Galatians 6:7 warns, "Be not deceived; God is not mocked: for whatsoever a man soweth, that shall he also reap."

This concludes the expositions of demons who had plagued the first 42 years of the life of our good friend Patty. Please do not think of her tormented life as somehow extraordinary. Quite to the contrary, it is typical of multitudes struggling to live an honorable Christian life but have not been taught the realities of demonic warfare as explained in these pages, and in the pages of the bible so carefully avoided by pastors and teachers. Opening of the mind to such knowledge brings with it the wondrous privilege of being delivered from secret, tormenting bondage.

Beyond those above, other folks suffering similar torments were also to find the same kind of help over the next four decades through our interventions. A significant number of believers received deliverance en mass at various public venues. Whether in private counsel or public meeting, however, the opportune time for such help is after the Holy Bible basis for deliverance has been presented and embraced: Teach and do, as Jesus did (Acts 1:1).

Previous pages and Book Two detail additional significant deliverances. Our idea for including them is to show specific features of deliverance that need to be learned by readers who feel led to engage. If questions have not been sufficiently answered in the foregoing, they will surely be addressed in pages that follow. For here is abundant, proven information that can lead to miraculous relief for the afflicted.

Parenthetically, someone anonymously uploaded to YouTube a 1970 testimony by Derek Prince. Having viewed it I heartily recommend its viewing for further edification. Access was "DEREK PRINCE – Amazing Testimony of Deliverance". If it is not still posted for viewing, possibly it could be found by searching. My takeaway near the end is when he states that the Lord told him specifically - in reference to teaching and demonstrating deliverance from demonic torments:

"I want it done in public, preached as a regular part of the gospel message; it is not to be treated as a secondary part of the ministry." In deference to such an Authoritative directive to him, that is exactly what we have done in print and in practice.

LAUNCH INTO MINISTRY

My personal deliverance from demons was initiated through Derek Prince, which profoundly changed my life and outlook forever. In eager anticipation I pursued classroom study under his teaching of basic bible doctrine. There was an open deliverance service every Friday evening. After two years I was convinced that the miraculous works he demonstrated would also operate through me. Belief was strong. Preparation was thorough in word and deed to carry a similar ministry to the church at large.

Derek Prince's expositions of the Holy Bible with miraculous demonstrations virtually shaped and clarified my faith, solidifying it into a righteous belief system. He opened the wonders of God's Word, which remain bedrock in my understanding and force. Thereafter, the Lord was faithful in allowing us to help liberate hundreds of victims in private sessions, small home groups, public meetings, and seminars in multiple states.

To support wife and children I was employed as executive vice president in a book and bible publishing company. Full time employment did not preclude personal deliverance ministry in the evenings, on weekends, and during vacations. No professional clerics were needed. Such dual endeavors – Christian business and miraculous deliverance – would thenceforth be incorporated into all future assignments, which prevails to the present.

It wasn't long before a "full gospel" organization recognized our work and formally ordained us for ever-expanding ministry. Heavens to Betsy! I do not like, but rather tolerate the title Reverend, because it is used only one time in the Holy Bible - Psalms 111:9 - to extol the virtues of God alone. Frankly I am embarrassed when someone asks, "Are you a reverend?" Yet, even the great Apostle Paul explained his adaptability, concluding in 1 Corinthians 9:19-22: "I am made all things to all men, that I might by all means save some." On that basis I nod yes to the few who ask.

I was born fourth of five sons of our Armenian immigrant father – an ordained Pentecostal minister, and American-born mother from Illinois. Dad had spotted her when, as an American soldier, he peered out the window of a moving troop train in 1917 World War One and threw out a note with his address. Five sons later proved that she knew what to do with it. In spite of their ignorance in this subject they were wonderfully faithful to preach salvation in Christ alone, individually gaining over 100 converts and many more through personally passing out more than a million tracts over 70 years.

Due to ignorance, the spiritual enemy was enabled to cause turmoil and conflict in our family. To escape the confusion, I had shut God and religion out of mind as intolerable and inexplicable. Over a quarter century I remained agnostic/atheistic, avoiding occasions that might call for reference to deity. God was dead to me.

CATALYST FOR CHANGE

The night after witnessing Patty's deliverance, at the end of Derek Prince's teaching I approached him. Though we had not been formally introduced and knowing he was already tired, I asked if he would grant me an appointment. He resisted the idea, saying with obvious impatience, "I'm not the only minister here - there are others in Chicago you could see." He lived in Florida but was in Chicago on a teaching assignment. With that rejection, he turned his back and walked away.

A deep-seated anger rose up as I watched him leave. Disappointment and a low-boiling rage flooded my mind at the rejection - another let down. Embarrassed that I had asked a mere human for a favor - especially a minister of Dad's religion, and angry with myself, I felt lesser and cheapened that I had showed weakness in breaking my vow of self-sufficiency.

Long before teen years, I had become emotionally hard and independent - a three-time runaway, only to be pursued by state police, repeatedly jailed, then returned again to our home "prison". Never asking help from anyone, I would steal before begging. Anger and hate were ever present. All my early life had developed under rejection, curse, mockery, poverty, demonic abuse, and witchcraft in lustful uncleanness at home. Living under constant threat laced with cruelty - all in the name of Christ, I could never have imagined its cause was demons, because I didn't even know demons or angels existed! More times than I could remember Dad cursed me with, "You rotten, hell-bound demon, you're not worth a damnable dime! No good, I'll knock the devil out of you first thing! You demon-possessed devil!"

Later adding, "You're of your father the devil!" He sometimes referred to his wife as "Devil Woman", which appeared to be justified. Verbal abuse was punctuated by a whipping with an unforgettable "rod of correction". Perhaps we could humorously say, "It left its mark". His curse carried the weight of spiritual authority - double in that he was my biological and legal father, I lived in his house, under his direct authority, where he was high priest.

We lived as a white-trash minority in a segregated, high-crime, black township in 1930's Missouri. Conflicts were common. Altogether these were my excuse for rebelling against religion and authority - of parents, law, police, as well as true and false gods which in collusion had destroyed the youthful innocence of five sons.

Father Flannigan's Home For Boys in Nebraska was too far out of reach. Application for a foster home was turned down by would-be foster parents, and Parole Officer Peter Sartorius told me, "They don't want you, either." The fires were being stoked. Rebellion was costly, and its price was going to be paid. But at least I could always depend upon myself to be 100% loyal and dedicated to me, to always act in my best interests! Alone I could have things my way. It takes the human mind but a split second of rubbing raw wounds to internally explode in a flash of violence. Here it all was, anger with a dark countenance exploding the very second Reverend Prince turned me down and walked away. Of course, it may be that he discerned my problem was a deep black hole that would be a waste of time to engage it. Later he said as much.

What was my scornful rationale? "But of course! What could a high-nose, privileged, only child of an aristocratic, military family, classically-educated British scholar – philosophy professor at Eton & Kings College at Cambridge, photographed among brilliants, Derek Prince - a mental don; what could he possibly know about somebody like me? We are a universe apart! The poor dumb cluck! His kind could never relate to real people! He just doesn't understand! His life is proper British pomp. What a laugh!"

But suddenly, after walking a few paces, Rev. Prince stopped at the exit, stood up straight a moment, as though listening to an order. Then he turned around, and in what seemed to be determined resignation, walked back to me. He leaned close and looked into my face. Quickly discerning my problem, he named it, saying "That's your problem isn't it." He wasn't asking but *telling* me. Surprised, I replied, "Problem?" Then he said, "Do you know God hates that?" In all honesty, I said, "Why NO!" Three months earlier I would have replied, "What God?" For I had absolutely no idea how God might have felt about my life. It just had not occurred to me because God had not been in my thoughts for twenty-five years. Quite to the contrary.

Sounding like a cop, Reverend Prince abruptly dictated his orders: "(1) Do not take any food (meaning I was to "fast") between now and tomorrow afternoon, (2) Start reading Psalms 25 and forward, making each of them your own prayer. (3) Come to my hotel room at 2:30 p.m. I'll try to help you."

I was glad but found it humorous, chuckling to myself, "007" big as life!" My mind was decompressing. He and I both had been trained in the military to instantly obey orders - right or wrong. I can still hear, "Yours is not to reason why; yours is but to do or die!" while lyrically drill marching two hours in cadence, "Hup ... one, two, three, four!"

He had served as medical orderly in the British Army in the North African Desert, and I in the United States Air Force in the South Pacific Islands. We were separated by two oceans, chains of islands, the entire North American Continent, and 7,000 miles – which, taken together approximated the distance between our "understandings". Suddenly it seemed comical that he had served in a military rank lower than mine as Staff Sergeant! Had we been serving in the same Unit he would be replying "Yes, Sergeant!" But now, in a different time and place, I nodded that I would obey his commands and keep the appointment. After all, to a General in the Army of God I had to concede that he now outranked me – musing that it appeared to be more British than American!

Arriving at his room next day, he motioned for me to sit on the straight-back chair, led me in a prayer professing faith in Christ, then began praying for me. After about 20 minutes of zero response, he and his wife, Lydia, excused themselves to keep another appointment, instructing me to continue praying while they were gone. They would return in half an hour.

Under a strange mental fog, I found myself unable to pray. My head bowed down, and I went to sleep. I didn't know how to continue alone, never having had this kind of experience. Twenty hours earlier I didn't even know that demons existed, still questioning whether words like demon and angel were merely bourgeoise vocabulary - like other slang words. Not helped, I had just stood up to leave when they returned.

Nothing they had hoped might happen actually did, as far as could be known. They recommended that I not give up but continue praying on my own. CRAP! Disillusioned and disappointed, I turned and walked out feeling a certain gritty hopelessness. There had been no evidence of any type of deliverance or change. Nothing. I was stuck with the same wretched, reliable me, dedicated to self-preservation, no matter what. Once again, I set the jaw, went back to basics, and as always, continued fighting an unknown evil.

PREPARATION BY DIVINE APPOINTMENT

It did seem suspiciously coincidental that 98 days earlier in Dallas, Texas, I had met Raymond H. Bloomfield, an evangelist from New Zealand, preaching at Souls Harbor Church. I was there on business with our Dallas Exchange Manager, Estelle Redd, who managed that region's film office. The last thing I could have expected was a supernatural encounter with God. The course of life that followed would have been unbelievable to me and deemed impossible at the time. It was to be profoundly more influential, broader in type and scope, than I could have dreamed. It soon led to meeting Derek Prince and learning the reality of the two spiritual kingdoms at war with each other. In a way, that still seems more like science fiction.

The date was March 13, 1965. Bloomfield was finishing his message on Saturday morning. A strange feeling came over me that made me weak, so unusual that, after the service I said to him, "Can I talk to you a minute?" palming him a 20-dollar bill. "I think I need to pray."

Immediately his face became serious. Looking up, as if seeing someone, his booming voice began to powerfully prophesy wondrous things. It was so humbling, and the anointing so powerful that I was crushed to the floor face down on the green shag carpet, covering my head with folded arms to shield from pulsing waves of power, imploring, "NO, God. NO!!" The feeling of deepest possible unworthiness was overwhelming. How could this be happening with my sinful, rebellious past?

Among the things proclaimed were: "Before you were conceived in your mother's womb I have called and chosen you to take my word to thousands of thousands." Other similar blessings with divine guidance were proclaimed, several details of which I don't fully remember ... perhaps due to shock. But altogether the experience was so emphatic that it was miraculously transformative. My sobbing in tears was uncontrollable, with such an overpowering that there could be no hint of self-consciousness. Truly, this was no ordinary religious experience! It was the most impactful thing that had ever happened, leaving me spiritually and emotionally ecstatic with wonder.

Reverend Bloomfield invited me to his upstairs church apartment, reserved for visiting evangelists. We shared in fellowship far above my class that evening. But the most startling part was his personal testimony of years earlier having been miraculously healed of incurable bone cancer by a holy angel. The heavenly messenger had simply materialized in his room, in physical body as a man.

He walked the few paces and sat on the edge of his bed. The weight of the angel's body pressed blankets down hard across Bloomfield's rotting legs, causing severe pain. Bloomfield winced and asked the messenger to please move a bit so as to relieve the pain. The angel obliged, just as any considerate man would, then forthrightly explained in a clear voice:

"**The Lord has heard your prayers and has sent me to bring healing to his servant. It is done**". His message was brief but colossal. Having completed his mission, he gracefully stood upright from sitting on the bed and gently dissolved to total invisibility. Bloomfield's legs were miraculously cured at that moment. Most amazing! I was euphoric. Though incredible to hear such a "science fiction-like" tale, I had been so energetically pre-conditioned that morning that I believed every word with a new and hopeful outlook, but without complete understanding.

It must be acknowledged that Ray Bloomfield himself was every bit as much angel to me as the visitor from heaven was to him. Actually, the word angel is defined *messenger*. Surely, he was that, having been placed by the Holy Spirit to resurrect me from spiritual death, and the literal angel sent to cure his body from untimely death. The main difference between the two is that the one again dissolved to invisible and immediately departed back to heaven, while Ray Bloomfield has remained a close associate of mine more than 52 years at this writing.

This was my introduction to the notion of angels being actual living, celestial entities who make round trips between heaven and earth on assignments to help the needy. Still reeling from this astounding, hardly-believable input, I returned to our headquarters in Chicago, where a few weeks later, Patty's even more staggering deliverance from 50+ demons was to be personally witnessed - myself even being an active participant! Here I was going from atheist to mentally grappling with supposed literal angelic and demonic beings in just thirteen weeks! Wondrous indeed!

Back to work in the down-to-earth film company, still pondering these mystical matters, I began talking about them.

AUTHOR'S BIOGRAPHY

A curious female colleague, Jean Godfrey Kovalcik - sister of television's Arthur Godfrey - said, "David, there's something different about you. What is it? Will you tell me?" She and my bride, Nancy, had become good friends visiting in her home. Meeting at a corner coffee shop I began telling of my outlandish encounters: one with the evangelist involving an angel, and the other about Patty's deliverance from demons.

Upon hearing such a preposterous tale, she burst into disbelieving laughter, but soon controlled herself enough to listen more courteously. She was obviously intrigued, but I couldn't help but notice the cute twinkling in her eyes while she patronized her friend.

Though not saying so, her demeanor told me she thought I was the same Hollywood fanatic on drugs still telling tales. True. I was somewhat drugged emotionally, and on a high with new supernatural experiences. I still am. What else could I say? It was all true - unbelievable, but true.

I knew they might think I was running off the rails, and even close friends might be skeptical. Who could blame them? They had known me for eight years as mentally earthbound. This new thing didn't compute. Had they challenged me I would not have been able to explain it either. All I was trying to tell them was that, suddenly, it seemed to appear that God might actually exist! But their unenlightened minds were not able to understand. Nor could I.

Referencing Matthew 13:19 and 1 Corinthians 2:14, "When anyone heareth the word of the kingdom, and understandeth it not, then cometh the wicked one, and catcheth away that which was sown in his heart." "But the natural man receiveth not the things of the Spirit of God; for they are foolishness unto him: neither can he know them, because they are spiritually discerned." This explains it. Blessed be the name of the Lord!

As I look back to those two pivotal days of March 13 and July 7, 1965, I shudder to think how bleak life would have been had those two servants of God not obeyed the Lord to discern my despair and intercede.

Today I know that after Prince turned his back and walked away, it was the Holy Spirit who caused him to stop and reconsider. Clearly his intention and actions had been to depart. Only then he turned around to offer me the brief appointment. There were undoubtedly a hundred others at that convention who would have wanted his personal attention. Those two meetings were singularly the most pivotal moments that turned my life from abject despair to joy in service to God over the next half century.

It had been a thunderous process involving two humble servants manifestly walking in divine guidance and power. As the Lord had arranged it, a productive relationship to Derek Prince Ministries and to Raymond Bloomfield Ministries was established and remains to this time.

By divine foreplan, Derek Prince had preached in Bloomfield's church in New Zealand, connecting their streams of ministry two years before I learned of it. There are no coincidences with God. The three of us were to become triune in spirit forever. Flowing out of our respective ministries the gospel of Jesus Christ has reached peoples of every continent, from Bloomfield's New Zealand; Prince's Jerusalem, Israel; and from our mid-America headquarters.

At Chicago's Faith Tabernacle six months later, Prince asked, "Brother, don't I know you from somewhere?" He had not remembered our brief appointment. I replied, "Why yes. Last July you prayed for me in your room at the Hilton Hotel." His next comment was so shocking it moved me to solemnity over the rest of my life. Thoughtfully and seriously he continued, "Oh yes, now I remember. I don't mind telling you, Brother, I frankly thought you were too far gone to be helped. You must be very grateful for what the Lord has done for you."

What a sobering jolt! I knew I needed help, even making numerous visits to psychologists and psychiatrists, but had no idea how close to damnation I was. Indeed, I must be the most grateful person you could ever meet. The merciful Lord preserved my life from eternity in hell!

Prayers which the Princes prayed in that brief appointment - which appeared to have no immediate effect - had, in fact, resulted in a real deliverance. It was proof that often a major deliverance occurs through prayer when there is no immediate outward evidence of it. Please absorb that fact, for the Lord works in unlimited ways beyond our understanding or expectation. Pray the Scriptures in faith, and then leave it in the Lord's hands.

Within two weeks, the pernicious problem I had endured from childhood, was unmistakably being cured - negative episodes quickly subsiding. Yet, it would require another six months to be essentially subdued, and two years to be altogether overcome. Within ten years that one and numerous other demonic strongholds - which, frankly, I had been blind to – had been unearthed and obliterated.

An unpleasant fact of Scripture applies now as then, shown by Apostle Paul's own difficulties: "For I know that in me [that is, in my flesh], dwelleth no good thing: for to will is present with me; but how to perform that which is good I find not." Noting Romans 7:18 -19, "For the good that I would I do not: but the evil which I would not, that I do." Verse 25b: " …So then with the mind I myself serve the law of God; but with the flesh the law of sin."

He further instructs us to bear the strains and to keep fighting for purity. In Hebrews 12:1b: " .... let us lay aside every weight, and the sin which doth so easily beset us, and let us run with patience the race that is set before us." Jeremiah 17:9 reveals, "The heart is deceitful above all things, and desperately wicked: who can know it?"

It thus appears that every believer is plagued with a besetting sin that requires continuing resistance for as long as it takes to obtain final victory. Most victims have learned by experience that to finally overcome entrenched sex-related sins, or nicotine and drug addictions, has only come at the end of a long, little-by-little struggle. Still, we always win if we keep resisting.

If the claims and information in this chapter raise questions in your mind, do not stop reading. The next chapters provide advice and helps that lead to miraculous recovery.

4

SIN AND ITS POWER

> *"... by one man sin entered into the world, and death by sin; and so, death passed upon all men, for that all have sinned." (Romans 1:12)*

As a young man I had flippantly used the word 'sin' many times and blindly participated in it for decades, though its definition had escaped me. At age 34, I asked Assembly of God Pastor Wallace Pearce, of Wilmette, Illinois, "What is sin? And why is it bad?" I am sure it sounded naïve, but it was a legitimate question that needed an answer. How else could I know? You may be honestly seeking the answer to that question too, because the natural mind is not able to comprehend it. Why? Because the natural mind itself is the very essence of sin: "…dead in trespasses and sin" (Ephesians 2:1). Everyone has been born into and bound by it.

Pastor Pearce's terse response was, "Sin is the transgression of the law…" of God (1 John 3:4). But how deep does sin go? What is its extreme? How bad is sin really? What is its importance today? Why would God be so angry with sin? Is there a remedy for it? From what must we be saved? How did it begin? Wasn't it 6000 years ago that it happened? Why should we be concerned?

A seemingly inconsequential act might be called a small sin, but it is inherently egregious. No matter the size, all sin is against God. In addition, some sins are also against man, and others can be against our own body (See 1Corinthians 6:18). On this latter basis alone, wisdom would dictate that we keep our bodies free from self-induced contamination beyond our original fallen nature. The late bible scholar Derek Prince would say, "That is just enlightened self-interest".

In order to better understand the term 'sin', a larger context is appropriate. First, "…Know ye not that…ye are not your own? Ye are bought with a price" (1 Corinthians 6:19-20). You have been bought and paid for with the blood of Jesus Christ! He is the legal Owner. Beyond that, Jeremiah 17:9 informs us, "The heart is deceitful above all things, and desperately wicked…" Again, in Genesis 6:5-7 our history is revealed: "And God saw that the wickedness of man was great in the earth, and that every imagination of the thoughts of his heart was only evil continually. And it repented the Lord that he had made man on the earth and it grieved him at his heart. And the Lord said, I will destroy man whom I have created from the face of the earth…". This was a cataclysmic response, giving us some notion of how vile sin is in God's opinion. While Noah was a sinner, he and his family were spared through grace because, as Pastor Jimmy Evans explains, he had not violated the human seed line as others had done, comingling the angelic with human species (Genesis 6:8 - See jimmyevans.org for elaborate treatment of this point).

What the Holy Bible calls sin encompasses indescribable degradation to such a degree that the offender must finally be cast into a burning hell, where, forever and ever, there is weeping, wailing, and gnashing of teeth (See Matthew 8:12 and Luke 13:27-28). From God's point of view, this is proper punishment; He alone decides the matter, and He is our Just Judge. There are no exceptions outside of those who respond to His offer of pardon. Were it otherwise, God would not have given the crowning jewel of heaven--His perfect Son, Jesus Christ, as the only acceptable sacrifice to redeem one who commits a sin. His cost was so great that man cannot comprehend it, for there is no earthly parallel. Thus, the greatest of all miracles is described in the single word salvation, from the single word sin.

Let us not be fooled by the simplicity of the language. It has infinite depth. Nothing else is one thousandth as important. His Word is so sure that, through the psalmist he said: "Thou hast magnified thy word above all thy name" [Psalm 138:2b], though it is above every other name in heaven and earth. And again, "Forever, O LORD, thy word is settled in heaven" (Psalm 119:89). Its cogency is such that one who commits a sin must "repent or perish" (See Luke 13:3). As for the pungent meaning of that warning, it would be understood after one has been judged and entered into either heaven or hell forever—with no option available. The time to obey is now. In Galatians 6:7 we are told: "Be not deceived; God is not mocked: for whatsoever a man soweth, that shall he also reap." It is less what we have done than the fact we are inherently born a sinner. Knowing this, who would dare be casual about sin and salvation?

We yet struggle against the terrible blight. There are terrors and pains—even to the ripping of kidney stones! The great saint of yesteryear, Smith Wigglesworth, said the pain of passing 200 kidney stones was the greatest trial of his life, as stated in his biography, Apostle of Faith. I have experienced only seven kidney stones …more than enough to confirm our brother's assessment!

Earth was a magnificent paradise specially designed for the joy of God's human offspring. Alas, both were lost. While sin had once occurred in heaven, there had never been a rescue, or salvation from its effect or of its perpetrator. Its penalty was swift and unalterable. Salvation was a new provision that would apply only to humans. Sin was so utterly destructive that it has required the massive, ongoing effort of God and man, to explain it in myriad ways. How inconceivable that a single, mere sin could be so deeply infused, inculcated, and laminated throughout the totality of natural man, and still not be understood, even while it consumes him! It takes a supernatural act of God to penetrate the unbelieving mind captivated by satanic sin.

Owing to its critical importance, our determination has been to sufficiently amplify its definition that it may be understood as the source of all human problems of every description, temporal and eternal. The hope is that it would begin to answer the gnawing doubts in every heart. Still, this is the lightest possible treatment of such a fundamental subject. The pages of this book unveil some of the emotional and fascinating interchanges between Almighty God, believers who love him, and the majority population who do not. The ongoing battles of believers to overcome the effects of this blight are without end.

We read in Habakkuk 1:13, "Thou art of purer eyes than to behold evil, and canst not look on iniquity…" Sin is so intolerable that God could not look upon it, even to the spurning of His only Son during his deepest possible agony, becoming sin for you and me, requiring his awful death by crucifixion. Jesus cried out to his Father, "Why hast thou forsaken me?" (See Matthew 27:46 and Mark 15:34) The answer to his question is: sin was so heinous, that it could not even be looked upon by Almighty God. Agonizing under the sin burden, Jesus did not live to see his 34th birthday. Our gratitude will first be seen by accepting the Lord's pardon freely offered; then by performing good works and obeying him forever to prove it.

Much credit goes to researcher Alexander Cruden, who worked three years in making Bible calculations before printing diverse facts. One set of facts is on page 344 of the 1981 edition of Crudens Concordance. He reveals that the King James translation of the Holy Bible is comprised of 66 books, 1189 chapters, 31,173 verses, 773,697 words and 3,566,480 alphabetic letters. All were written in longhand on parchment scrolls over the 13 centuries 1200 B.C. to 95 A.D. Its forty scribes lived on three continents, to whom the words were dictated infallible by their Author. Even after thousands of years of truth and consequences in evidence, the majority of humans refuse to believe in Christ, only to receive their legally-required, earned wages of eternal damnation. Such is the grisly grasp of this unyielding three-letter word—sin.

"For I am not ashamed of the gospel of Christ: for it is the power of God unto salvation to everyone that believeth..." (Romans 1:16). Salvation from what? Sin and its consequences, temporal and eternal. Sin is the power of Satan, whether anyone believes it or not. Apart from the few being saved, every human on earth has already been consumed in sin's grip to utter and total destruction. While we breathe, sin's tentacles suck the vitality and life out of every part of soul and body in our struggle to stay alive. It is so pernicious and all-consuming that no earthly power can loosen its lock.

How sad that a comparative few will believe the gospel of Christ and be saved from the inescapable consequence of sin (See Matthew 7:14). All others are so blinded by its contamination that their eyes will never be opened. Having refused the grace of God they are bound for utter destruction, to live forever in the torments of living death (see Luke 16:23-31).

The gospel of Christ is the most vaunted theme of the Holy Bible. In fact, it is the only purpose for the bible's existence. Every story, admonition, law, ordinance, and example on every page points only to the gospel. For it alone can prevent one's ruination. That fact inversely reveals the power of sin—Satan's domain. All forms of religion, except the pure gospel of Jesus Christ, merely "rearranges the deck chairs on a sinking ship", as one has said. Few are saved; most are lost.

ARMAGEDDON OF THE FLESH

"The soul that sinneth, it shall die" (Ezekiel 18:14 + 20). So also, must the body, even though both were designed to live forever without need of a fix. Throughout Scripture such terms as "filthiness of the flesh, fleshly, carnal, put off the old man and his deeds" are found among many others. While created in the image and likeness of God the Son, by God the Son Himself, later passages inform us that we must the second time be conformed to the image of his dear Son (Romans 8:29). What happened?

The physical flesh had been as fully decimated as the soul. We are presented with warnings and examples of the wicked soul and body, co-conspirators against God. Ironically, they are the most coveted, desirable, and effective vehicles available for Satan's demons to inhabit. Through them he is able to steal, kill, and utterly destroy most of the creatures God ever created. And even the few souls that are saved must undergo voluntary self-destruction in order to be re-created into new beings fit for heaven.

"Therefore, if any man be in Christ, he is a new creature: old things are passed away; behold, all things are become new" (2 Corinthians 5:17b). The satanic destruction of the human body and soul at the first was so complete that no part of them could ever enter into God's heavenly abode. The souls and bodies that are not recreated and conformed to the image of the Son of God are finally to be cast into hell with Satan.

From the beginning until now, human history shows the nature of the selfish soul and flesh in action. Their expression is largely religious in one form or another, in obeisance to one god or another, even if it is self-worship. All cultures, generation by generation, have followed the same annihilating course toward Sodom and Gomorrah, ending in self-destruction. In modern times, such a display is telecast 24 hours a day without interruption. It is because Satan's powerful influence and shackles are so total over man that Jesus rightly says to us, "…Without me ye can do nothing" (John 15:5).

Yet, compared to the "all power and authority" of Jesus, Satan's "much power" is little. When compared to man's "powerless" slavery, however, Satan's power is total. He indeed is "god of this world, prince of darkness, prince of the power of the air." Taken together these titles embody both the earth realm and the lower heavens. This is why, even the great angelic prince of God—Michael the Archangel, "dared not bring a railing accusation against Satan when contending for the body of Moses, but said, rather, The LORD rebuke thee" (Jude 1:9).

If you have any doubt about the weakness of man compared to the power of Satan, try casting demons out of a human demoniac in *your own name, power, and authority*. In so doing, be assured that your experience will mirror that of another who attempted to do so! Read it for yourself in

Acts 19:14-19. The seven sons of Sceva made the attempt, but were beaten up, bruised, wounded, and thrown out of the house naked by the demon!" The demon was neither disturbed nor cast out.

Read about my own futile attempt to deliver a person in my own strength. It is my account of a young man named Stacy. I was an eager Christian at the time, though obviously a little careless and cocky from earlier successes. It was the mercy of the Lord that kept me from being overthrown. After hours of perspiration and failure, I finally and truly called upon the Lord, who taught me an unforgettable lesson in a shocking display. What I could not do in nine exhausting hours, the Lord did within two seconds! Read the Case titled *Stacy and the Roaring Lion* in Book Two.

The foregoing is a long answer to the short question posed, and I wish it had been explained to me as it is here. Let the last word on the matter be a few verses of Scripture, which is the supreme authority for us all:

"For the wages of sin is death; but the gift of God is eternal life through Jesus Christ our Lord" (Romans 6:23).

"For all have sinned and come short of the glory of God" (Romans 3:23).

"The Lord ... is longsuffering ... not willing that any should perish, but that all should come to repentance" (2 Peter 3:9).

"For God so loved the world, that he gave his only begotten Son, that whosoever believeth in him should not perish, but have everlasting life" (John 3:16).

"That if thou shalt confess with thy mouth the Lord Jesus, and shalt believe in thine heart that God hath raised him from the dead, thou shalt be saved. For with the heart man believeth unto righteousness; and with the mouth confession is made unto salvation" (Romans 10-9-10).

More than mere hope, it is a fact that when you honestly confess your belief as shown in the last verse above, even a mind blinded by sin will be divinely opened to comprehend the marvels revealed in these pages. If you have doubts about that, you may qualify your confession by praying, "Lord, if you show me you exist, I will confess it as above shown." Do not lie.

It is said, "The mills of justice grind slowly but grind exceedingly fine." As no one ever escapes judgment in the end, I implore you to make your profession of faith while it is possible, for there is no guarantee that you will be alive tomorrow.

It is noteworthy that the word 'sin' is rarely mentioned in the news reports of secular radio, television, newspapers, magazines, or the internet. Violations of propriety and laws are identified, but never their underlying cause or biblical identity. They are the spirits (demons) of murder, mayhem, rape, arson, stealing, cheating, and corruption, to name a few. Throughout the bible however, sins are named and explained, and clearly defined. Not all, but many are listed in the following pages. While all of us are guilty, there is still time to repent—but little time. Why not take that moment right now? Why would you not? "My spirit shall not always strive with man" (Genesis 6:3), which makes it perilous to hesitate. Once the Holy Spirit withdraws, one's doom is sealed.

5

WARFARE DECREE

"...decree a thing and it shall be established." (Job 22:28)

DECREE FOR FAMILY AND PROPERTY

This decree proved to be effective in turning a near disaster into a blessing. It had come through intense frustration from a truly demonized tenant family who were severely damaging our rental property 700 miles away. No husband was to be found. The lady, with two small and inordinately beautiful children, was intermittently living in adultery with an unrelated married man, who also gave her money. Illegal drugs were involved in the whoredom as well.

Angry at the devil, I sought the Lord for an answer. This decree is what He gave me. I wrote it on paper before driving to Houston, confronting the family, then declaring this warfare decree while walking through the premises. When all rooms had been covered, I placed the document inside the attic as a permanent testimony. Thereafter, from anywhere in the world

I could confidently remind the Lord of its presence and ask that He dispatch a warring angel to enforce its provisions. This gave me wonderful assurance. The result was so positive that I repeated placing the Decree in other properties. Each and every one of them became profitable because of the Decree.

Demons who remain in a property vacated by previous tenants are called "Squatter Spirits." This term is borrowed from a history book that describes folks who, though not authorized, secretly took refuge in a vacant property, and acted as though they were the owners.

A word of caution is needful: This decree works only for believers in Jesus Christ. I advise against its use by non-believers, lest a negative effect occur. Read about such a thing happening in Acts 19:13-16.

This decree is to be declared aloud in a commanding voice while walking through each room of the property. When the declaration has been completed, physically place the printed decree on the property as a permanent testimony. My placement is usually in the attic.

DECREE FOR HOUSE AND HOUSEHOLD

Our Father and our God, we thank you that we who have asked your Son Jesus Christ to save our souls have the privilege of coming boldly before you, just as a child may boldly come to his parent. We believe the Holy Bible to be your true Word. In 1 Chronicles 29:11 and 13, You tell us that You have the greatness, power, glory, victory, and majesty: and all that is in heaven and in earth is yours. It is your Kingdom, O Lord, and you are exalted as head above all. "Now therefore, our God, we thank thee and praise thy glorious name."

You also say in Luke 10:19-20. Behold, I give unto you power to tread on [evil spirits called] serpents and scorpions, and over all the power of the enemy; and nothing shall by any means hurt you."

Therefore, to carry out this authority here today on behalf of the Kingdom of God, and in agreement with these witnesses, it is hereby decreed:

That this property, known as our household—inside and outside, land, buildings, inhabitants and animals—are now taken from the satanic spiritual enemy as a spoil of war, and that these are hereby dedicated to the Lord Jesus Christ. This place is set apart and made holy by our testimony, through the Blood of Jesus Christ. From today forward, all persons in full agreement with this spiritual decree shall be blessed in accordance with this decree.

IT IS FURTHER DECREED:

That through this act of dedication, every present evil spirit, whether named or not named, must bow to Divine authority, and must now vacate these premises, and depart from its owners and tenants, by order of the Lord Jesus Christ, through us.

We break every curse inherited from previous occupants, every curse from antiquity against property and family, whether inherited generational curse, whether upon family through addictions, poverty, disease, deformity, the occult, or by iniquity. We tell you that Jesus Christ took all curses upon Himself on the Cross for us. Therefore, all curses are hereby returned to those who placed them.

As you have no rights, neither part nor lot in this matter—and no ability to resist—you will obey us, as we are the redeemed of the Lord, for we are many. There is no salvation for you evil spirits; you will be forever cast into hell by the Lord Jesus Christ.

NOW, Satan, we address you directly:

We call forth all spirits not of God—foul spirits who cause property damage, blight, disease and death; pest and pestilence; clutter and junk; neglect and intrusion, worry, fear, theft, want, and insufficiency: We command you to desist and expire in your works of wickedness.

You unclean spirits of Poverty, Pornography, Rape, Incest, Sexual Uncleanness, Evil Imaginations, Lasciviousness, Adultery, Lust and Lust of the Eyes; spirits of Battery, Child Abuse, Shame, and Worry. You are commanded to vacate these premises, its owners and occupants.

You demon forces of Rebellion, Rejection, Unforgiveness, Hate, Anger, Violence, Misery, Murder, and Retaliation, Nicotine, Drunkenness; Drug Addiction, Lying and Deception, Spirits of Occult: Ouija, Witchcraft; False Religions; and all kindred spirits --

Uproot yourselves now as we come against you through the blood of Jesus Christ, by the anointing of the Holy Spirit, on the authority of the Word of God.

You are ordered to abate, expire and desist your operations in this property, its owners and occupants, including animals.

We now loose the holy angels and implore the Lord to engage in this battle on behalf of ourselves in the kingdom of God, on the basis of Hebrews 1:14 and Matthew 18:19.

Now, having made this proclamation before Almighty God, in the presence of witnesses, as it is written, so let it be done. In the mighty name of Jesus. Amen.

Note: I recommend that you either photograph or copy this decree and print it for permanent deposit in your building(s), rather than tear out book pages.

Decree for The Nations:

We further decree that 100,000 centers of Witchcraft be destroyed in the year 2019. Their curses are returned upon their heads. Locations begin with our town, extending to New York City, NY., Washington D.C., Philadelphia, PA., Chicago, IL., Houston-Dallas-Fort Worth, TX., Salt Lake City, UT., Las Vegas, NV., San Diego- Los Angeles-San Francisco-Sacramento, CA., Seattle, WA., and Portland, OR.

Amen

6

COINCIDENCE IS NOT BIBLICAL

We must presume it is the Lord who draws us to read biblical truth. In Psalm 37:23 we read, "The steps of a good man are ordered of the Lord." Doubtless, you are reading this book by the will of God. Likely you are considering its implications for your life, as it provides a considerable amount of information not commonly taught. Even so, head knowledge alone is not enough to cause us to act in ways that are holy. Scripture facts must become experiential if they are going to be lived and convincingly demonstrated to others. Our desire is that this process might become complete in you and through you to others.

It is required that we look at ourselves in the mirror of Scripture. Any wickedness that is discovered must be discarded, whether generated by our self-nature alone, or amplified by intrusion of an evil spirit. In this section we are examining how we can more fully develop the new creation Christ made of us at the new birth (i.e. when "born again"). To achieve it will require that we deal a death blow to our carnal nature – the one exploited by our spiritual enemies. My personal experience and confirming scriptures are the basis for our discussion.

While everyone is born dead in spirit by reason of original sin, that death is overcome in the "new birth". Born again means that our spirit is restored by Jesus Christ, for the purpose of refurbishing and nurturing our corrupted soul back to health, vitality, and maturity. As with natural birth, growth to maturity is a long process. The new birth does not mean you are reborn a glorious, finished, and mature child of God. It means that the door to an exciting walk with God has opened. Its pathway is narrow and fraught with threats that must be avoided or overcome. Former propensities of selfishness are to be obliterated little by little, through our working partnership with the Savior. If a demon has invaded our soul he must be identified, overcome and expelled by force of warfare, using the superpower weapons described in Ephesians 6.

The Old Testament gives us a shadow or type of right strategy. Literal Canaan land that "flowed with milk and honey" is a type of our abundant life in New Testament salvation. Exodus 23:27-30 has been quoted in previous pages. Using that analogy, Canaan is where we are walking right now. Joshua, leader of the Israelites, died at the age of 110, having conquered most of Israel's enemies. But five heathen kingdoms remained in Canaan and had to be destroyed before godly occupation would be complete.

Similarly, multitudes of Christians live godly lives doing battle, but pass away before experiencing full and complete deliverance. I am a little uneasy in admitting that my experience is similar to that of Joshua. As a personal example, though matured in years, I still find it difficult to love enemies who aim to destroy me. Yet Jesus requires us to love our enemies. Whether that failing is demonically inspired or is the corrupted nature acting up, is not the vital question. Both are involved. I must deal with it.

If indeed a demon is its inspiration, he must be evicted. For me to genuinely love my enemies would qualify as a major deliverance! Failure to adjust, however, would mean loss on judgment day - not hell, but forfeiture of rewards, such as favored status and crowns, which obedience would have earned.

The need for deliverance ministry in all its forms is undeniable because diverse bondages such as addiction, disease, pain, and desire for wrongdoing are an obvious reality. Nor is deliverance to be considered a one-time event. If that declaration seems foreboding, do not be stumbled. By the time you have read to the conclusion of this book, one miracle will already have occurred. The Lord would have illumined your mind and made you eager to have the bible's wondrous promises fulfilled in your life.

For a believer in need, help is available by calling the telephone numbers provided on the Resources page of this book. You may call and explain what you have read, then ask them to confirm its truth and pray on your behalf. Then go to your pastor. Inform him or her of the examples and lessons in this book. Have him or her pray for your deliverance according to the scriptures and the instructions provided here. If he is unwilling, again call the resource contacts and ask them to refer you to a knowledgeable deliverance minister. The Lord will direct you. Never give up, because "Thanks be unto God which ALWAYS causeth us to triumph in Christ…" (2 Corinthians 2:14a).

For some matters it is proper to make a "time-certain", semi-formal appointment with the Lord, quite like agreeing to meet with any person of high standing. This allows you time to thoroughly prepare in prayer, fasting, and study with clear focus on the specific hour you and the Lord agreed upon. [Yes, knowing your need, the Lord agreed].

True deliverance comes from Jesus to all who embrace his sacrifice on their behalf. It is for those who believe on him, confess his name, and live as best they can, according to the scriptures. This is the salvation process. On the other hand, all who have rejected Jesus Christ as personal Lord and Savior, are already condemned. If they never accept him, they finally will be cast into the hell that was prepared for the devil and his angels. That terrible place is big enough to contain all rebels forever. That is the provision of Scripture – the Book of the Law (Psalm 9:17; Revelation 21:8). Rejecting the Holy Spirit's leading to Jesus Christ is the ultimate and unforgivable blasphemy.

Through Jesus Christ alone come all the blessings upon God's people: physical healing "…with his stripes we are healed" (Isaiah 53:5); our spirit is reconnected to God's Spirit. He alone provides deliverance from the power of sin, the devil, and his emissaries. Deliverance from demonic power is a benefit of salvation, as are healing and baptism in the Holy Spirit. All who come to Jesus qualify, but without Him you have no such privileges. "Every good gift and every perfect gift is from above, and cometh down from the Father of lights ..." (James 1:17). But once forgiven, Jesus said, "Behold, thou art made whole: sin no more lest a worse thing come upon thee" (John 5:14).

AUTHENTIC VS. FAKE MIRACLES

There is genuine deliverance, and there is a counterfeit deliverance. As "god of this world", Satan can order an evil spirit to temporarily depart from his victim to achieve a deceptive purpose. If he does that, he has an ulterior motive of something worse for that person. Satan also has the power to cause or invoke sickness upon a person, and to withdraw that sickness to make it appear the person was healed. If healing does not come through Jesus Christ, it will not stand. Demons are subject to Satan's decrees and commands. Likewise, Satan is subject to God and to obedient Christians who act in the authority given us by Jesus, through the power of the Holy Spirit.

FALSE ACCUSATION

In Matthew 12: 22-27, Jesus was accused of healing by satanic power: "Then was brought unto him one possessed with a devil, blind, and dumb: and he healed him, insomuch that the blind and dumb both spake and saw." At verse 24 an accusation against Jesus is stated: "This fellow doth not cast out devils, but by Beelzebub the prince of the devils." In verse 26 Jesus rebuffed: "And if Satan cast out Satan, he is divided against himself; how shall then his kingdom stand?" Verse 28: "But if I cast out devils by the Spirit of God, then the kingdom of God is come unto you." This narrative is repeated in Luke 11:15-20.

Once a spirit has been expelled, the believer should verbally ask the Holy Spirit to fill the void – that is, occupy the "room" where the evil spirit had previously lived. Jesus warned that an unclean spirit who was evicted, shall return and try again to take up his old residence. Let us look at the further explanation in Luke 11:24-26, also reported in Matthew 12:43-45. "When the unclean spirit is gone out of a man, he walketh through dry places, seeking rest; and finding none, he saith, I will return unto my house whence I came out. And when he cometh, he findeth it swept and garnished [clean and furnished]. Then goeth he, and taketh to him seven other spirits more wicked than himself; and they enter in, and dwell there; and the last state of that man is worse than the first."

Here we see that evil spirits [demons] are unclean. Some are declared to be "more wicked" than others. Jesus explains that when spirits are forced to vacate a person's body the demons suffer. They have no rest outside a body because they cannot overtly express their evil character in thin air alone. On the outside, that is all "the poor devils" have – thin air!

DEMONS AND JESUS KNOW EACH OTHER

All ranks of invisible beings know and testify of Jesus Christ, as shown in the three examples below. Look at the account in Mark 5:1-20: Verses 6 and 7 inform us that a demon knew Jesus at a distance: "But when he saw Jesus afar off, he ran and worshiped him, And cried with a loud voice, and said, What have I to do with thee, Jesus, thou Son of the most high God?" The same account at Luke 8:28 reports: "When he saw Jesus he cried out, and fell down before him, and with a loud voice said, what have I to do with thee, Jesus, thou Son of God most high? I beseech thee, torment me not."

In Acts 19:14-16 there was an evil spirit in the presumptuous son of a Jewish priest named Sceva. "And the evil spirit answered and said, Jesus I know, and Paul I know; but who are ye? And the man in whom the evil spirit was leaped on them (more than one person), and overcame them, and prevailed against them, so that they fled out of that house naked and wounded."

At Matthew 4:3 Satan went to Jesus and said: "If thou be the Son of God, command that these stones be made bread." There were temptations and conversation between Satan and Jesus, initiated by Satan. When he was known as Lucifer in heaven, he tried to overthrow the Lord. They were well acquainted but did not remain friends after Lucifer's betrayal.

DISPOSITION AND RELOCATION OF EVICTED DEMONS

When evil spirits are cast out, where do they go? They do not want to remain outside a body. In order to find rest, they will seek another human in which to live and act out their unsalvageable, evil, depraved, and wicked character. God has elected not to offer them a way of salvation, regardless of rank, ranging from archangel Lucifer, to fallen angels, to demons.

TWO THOUSAND DEMONS IN ONE MAN

Notice the example of the legion of spirits cast out of the "demoniac of Gadara". (The ruling Roman legions were comprised of 2,000 to 6,000 soldiers.) In Mark 5:1-20 the Legion of evil spirits asked Jesus' permission to go into a herd of swine, whereupon Jesus said, "Go." They went out of the man and into the bodies of the pigs. Of course, all the pigs immediately went berserk, ran violently into the sea and drowned. Upon the death of the pigs, the spirits were again released, this time from the bodies of swine. Spirits do not die but remain alive to actively seek new habitation inside believers where possible. They prefer humans because their body and soul are the most complex of all living creatures. Once inside, they can better exploit the wonderful complexities to do the most damage to the individual, his family, and to the kingdom of God.

WAYS IN WHICH THE LORD BRINGS DELIVERANCE

As Creator and Sovereign of the cosmic universe and its inhabitants, the Lord knows the condition and needs of our heart. He effects deliverances in every form and manner. I have personally received multiple deliverances in just about every scriptural way. In one case a demon being expelled gave a protracted high-pitched squeal while repeatedly stomping my left foot on the floor. The involuntary stomping was in some way tied to the squealing, though I do not know the connection. Forty-two years later I am questioning why my left leg and foot - the same one that stomped - later began intermittently to swell with edema.

An observation is that, while still infant in a crib, a rat chewed a substantial hole in my left ankle. At age 5 a leg was broken; at age 7 a nail replacing a bolt on a bicycle ripped a hole in the calf of the left leg. At age 10 a rusty nail protruding vertically from a board punctured the arch of my foot when I stomped on it during a barefoot run. At about the same time, I fell from a tree. Episodes of trauma and shock give opportunity for a spirit to enter in. Whenever we state such a fact to a medical doctor, it usually evokes a patronizing smile. Little does he know that biblical truth is stranger than fiction, and is, in fact, the original source perverted to the farce of modern science fiction!

On the occasion of this deliverance, I had made a precise appointment with the Lord and His servant, missionary Cas Knoester, who was visiting from Kenya, Africa to Dallas,

Texas. My wife was present with several others. Two weeks earlier, Brother Knoester had said to me, "You name the time and the day, and the Lord will meet you there." I named the day and time and kept the appointment. Because that meeting was so effective and exactly "on schedule", it taught me the unforgettable lesson that God honors our specific appointments with him, sometimes weeks in advance. There was no question of me keeping the appointment because I had the need. But the idea that God would keep an appointment set by me was new– and most precious. Think about that!

The name of the stomping, squealing demon was Pretense, and with him were five others. All six were cast out within half an hour. Pretense had penetrated and solidified his position in me during my eight years employment in the "pretense industry" - Hollywood entertainment films, which we distributed all over the world.

On another occasion, in Evanston, Illinois, there was a dramatic night vision, in which the Lord cast seven spirits out of me. They were ejected merely by me reaching out and touching his fingers, as his dead body lay on a stretcher being carried past me in a funeral procession. Those spirits came roaring out of me, made a U-turn and immediately tried to come back! I saw their shapes and woke up in a sweat. It was late in the night. I began to battle them with everything I had. I screamed, "NO! NO! It was a sovereign deliverance and a battle to prevent their return. I won!

My wife, Nancy, was startled awake by the loud yelling, of course! That mess took some explaining to her, but it helped that I was jubilant! In spite of her thinking I was "crazy", she knew I was sincere, and our marriage lasted another 50 years before she left me to join the angels in heaven.

Again, when I was still new in my experience with the Lord, Derek Prince prayed for me. I tried to cooperate as best I knew how but had no manifestation whatever. It seemed that nothing had happened. Within two weeks, however, I knew I had had a tremendous deliverance because my life changed dramatically in the area that had been most problematic. The change was so dramatic it was undeniable. I knew it and so did our company employees, who said so.

Another variation came during an anointed praise service one Sunday morning at Faith Tabernacle, in Chicago. Brother Derek Prince quickly stepped up to the microphone during the height of the praise and began to exhort the people saying, "You can have your healing now! This is the moment for your deliverance! The Spirit of Deliverance has come. Claim it right now." In full cooperation, over the next four minutes, I received deliverance from four spirits. There was a distinctive belch with each expulsion. The release was obvious.

You do not have to belch or cough. Physical reactions are not a requirement. Deliverance does not happen the same way every time. But please be clear on one point. If, in the course of seeking deliverance, your body wants to scream or stomp or belch, do not hold it back or you will be holding back your deliverance. The demon inside of you cannot come out unless you let him out!

God can arrange it any way He chooses. My overall experience with deliverance has been that a physical manifestation occurs 99% of the time. Beyond the above-named manifestations, there have been two occasions of different ladies slithering across the floor hissing as a serpent, with rattling in the throat that sounded like a rattlesnake; others falling on the floor, vomiting, screaming, roaring like a lion, a man in a restaurant meowing like a tomcat, you name it. I have seen it happen just as it is described in the pages of your bible.

Study the examples of deliverance in the scriptures. When you read them one after the other, you will soon believe it is true. Not every demon Jesus dealt with was quiet or behaved. Most of the deliverances he effected in his public ministry were of the kind I just described. They were loud and violent - and that is what we may expect in some cases.

Unlike pet animals, demons cannot be trained or forced to behave. There are certain limitations you can put on them, but you cannot make them into gentlemen. They cannot and will not behave; it is not in their nature. They will not act contrary to their evil nature, except when pretending for the purpose of deceiving. Genesis 3:1-5 is the prime and first example of that, when Satan deceived Eve.

PHYSICAL ASPECTS OF DELIVERANCE

Some ladies have said their deliverance experience was quite like giving birth to a baby. It required protracted hard pushing and pain. Evil spirits often reside down low in the bowel area of the human body where there is more room, comparatively speaking. There they hide, making it their habitation. This is especially so when spirits have been imbedded a long period of time – perhaps decades.

LAYING ON OF HANDS

There is a "mechanical" side of ministry as well as the spiritual side. Ministry often includes the laying on of hands for impartation of healing, ordination, blessing and commissioning one to a mission field or to special service. It was true of the early apostles and remains valid today. Laying on of hands imparts "something". When dealing with evil spirits, we impart the substance of faith (Hebrews 11:1).

They must and do respond in proportion to the faith imparted against them. Not all deliverance ministry requires the personal laying on of hands. The Holy Spirit has no limits or special rituals. However, this practice has extensive precedent. In one-on-one ministry I follow the precedents and always lay hands on the candidate for the impartation.

Demons are not much bothered by words alone. They have withstood words without power for centuries. Immune to blustering religious words, they carry on their devilish work largely unhindered. However, when forceful commands are given under the anointing and power of the Holy Spirit, they are overwhelmed and have no choice but to obey. Power is the substance of faith, which is the substance of "things hoped for".

Babes in Christ speak many loud words with little effect. It is the anointing of power that breaks the yoke. Isaiah 10:27 says that the burden of "…the yoke shall be destroyed because of the anointing."

Acts 1:8

"But ye shall receive power, after that the Holy Ghost (Holy Spirit) is come upon you."

Acts 2:43

"And fear came upon every soul: and many wonders and signs were done by the apostles."

Mark 16:17

"And these signs shall follow them that believe (all believers); In my name they shall cast out devils (demons)."

Acts 6:6

"Whom they set before the apostles (Stephen and others): and when they had prayed, they laid their hands on them." Deacons received divine blessing for future service.

Acts 19:6

"And when Paul laid his hands upon them, the Holy Ghost (Spirit of God) came on them; and they spake with tongues and prophesied." (Impartation of the Holy Spirit to believers in Ephesus)

2 Timothy 1:6

"Wherefore I put thee in remembrance that thou stir up the gift of God, which is in thee by the putting on of my hands." (A gift of God was imparted to Timothy.)

James 5:14

"Is any sick among you? Let him call for the elders of the church; and let them pray over him, anointing him with oil in the name of the Lord." (Hands apply the symbolic anointing oil for healing of the sick.)

Luke 13:11-13

Jesus laid his hands on a woman who had an infirmity, to impart healing and deliverance from a demon who had held her bent over in physical bondage eighteen years.

Leviticus 16:21-22

"And Aaron shall lay both his hands upon the head of the live goat, and confess over him all the iniquities of the children of Israel…and the goat shall bear upon him all their iniquities…" (This was transference of sin/guilt to an innocent scapegoat by the laying on of hands)

Numbers 27:18-19 and 23

"And the Lord said unto Moses, take thee Joshua…and lay thine hand upon him…and give him a charge (responsibility) in their sight. And he laid his hands upon him, and gave him a charge as the Lord commanded..." (Consecrating Israel's new leader)

Repeating for emphasis, a babe in Christ may say all the right words and get little results, while someone mature in Christ with few words, can impart his tried and true faith and forcefully remove the demon. This is not an iron-clad rule.

The laying on of hands imparts against the spirits directly. With experience and by discerning we impart the substance of faith to force their departure from wherever they cling. Proximity of participants bears upon the results. Closeness presents a stronger stream of faith. Sometimes a spirit will scream in agony and keep moving to different parts of the body because your impartation includes invisible fire of the Holy Spirit, rather like a flamethrower. The words: "Stop! You're killing me! Flames! Fire!" sometimes are screamed by the demons.

Impartation is a literal, real, divine substance that is Spirit, it is fire, it is pressure and it forces the demons to move. They cannot long stand against it, but it may take from minutes to an hour to complete the deliverance.

Within the bounds of decency, especially in ministry to the opposite gender, be sure to ask permission before laying a hand on someone's body. This applies when a demon is hiding in a somewhat private sector. In such a case, have the candidate place their hands appropriately, having yours atop theirs. Often their participating spouse may be helpful. If there is any question of propriety, just command by words in faith. The Holy Spirit is "an understanding gentleman".

Consider that the word "spirit" (*pneuma* in Greek) literally is breath, wind, air. If you blow up a balloon with air, you can see that the air is a substance that will be housed and conformed in the shape of the balloon. It is real and literal. It exists. Now consider the size and substance of a demonic spirit. Some are larger and stronger than others. From the lower region of the body, they can move about and conform to the shape of the particular "container" they target – such as hands, fingers, or vertebrae, where arthritis may be established. If the target is the brain, that is where he may cause confusion, migraine headache, tumor, epilepsy, or palsy.

One spirit might dwell in the nose – the air-spirit passageway to the lungs, where he can generate asthma, bronchitis, or other pulmonary diseases. Alternately, he may just be the doorkeeper to permit other spirits to enter through the passage to do damage. Another in the finger or vertebrae to cause arthritis. This is a common mode of their activity. Typically, one demon torments one part of the body. In the case at Luke 8:26-39 and Mark 5:1-18, reporting on "the demoniac at Gadara," the takeover was almost total. That *possession* required a legion of demons (from 2,000-6,000), under the headship of a "strongman" - the spokesman for the whole "battalion". Even with all that, the victim survived.

In John 5:15 Jesus says, "...without me ye can do nothing."
But without us Jesus will do nothing more.

When Jesus asked the spirit, "What is your name?" it wasn't to learn new information about demons for Himself. As Creator God, he knew all things from "the beginning". The purpose of the question was to reveal the nature and facts of a major deliverance, which his disciples could later replicate. It was a demonstration for us to follow in later practice – like right now!

No single demon can match the power or totally control the superior personality of a human. They can surreptitiously invade only a small part of the body and control its function to a large extent.

Applying physical pressure is somewhat similar in a spiritual sense to surrounding or squeezing the air in a balloon. If you depress one spot the air is compressed, causing it to move away from the pressure point. The same principle helps the deliverance candidate do what is otherwise more difficult.

It can sometimes be physically almost impossible to deliver yourself. The minister helps the candidate deliver that thing. As to where to place ministering hands, I usually place one hand on the forehead and the other at the low back. That imparts spiritual power and physical pressure into two main areas of residence.

Manifestations of the demons will determine more actions. If you compress against that little pocket of evil air, it has to go somewhere. That place is up! It will go out the respiratory system opposite the direction it came in. When the candidate breathes out with gusto, it helps move the spirit into the outgoing stream of air. Do not be surprised if other expulsions of air also are experienced. The spirit must be expelled with pressure.

When it comes to the throat part of the exit – narrower than the previous dwelling place – you have the same size air "pocket" being compressed into a smaller place than where it had been. That is what causes the coughing and retching in the throat. As the spirits move upward, you trace your pressure against them. You are to impart against them all the way through full expulsion. Otherwise they can fool you by becoming inert and silent. That is their tricky, last ditch effort to sneak back into hiding inside. Spirits exit one at a time.

I have yet to deal with a person whose deliverance was only one spirit. It has always been two or more. Jesus referred to "wolves in sheep's clothing", which typifies multiple demons as in a wolf pack. Moreover, "two or three banding together" is a principle of more power developed in combination, both for them and for us.

PRACTICAL DISCERNING

On the matter of discerning, it is not so mysterious as many believe. It is not entirely mystical or supernatural. You know the nature of a spirit by its fruit. The Lord says, "Ye shall know them by their fruits…" (Matthew 7:16). If you see a person who acts in a way that matches the description or name of an evil spirit, that conduct would be suspect in the natural. Knowing the scriptures helps our discerning.

God acts supernaturally upon the natural, somewhat like super-imposing upon us as we act together. You see with your eyes, hear with your ears, and smell with your nose. These senses in large part help in the discerning of spirits. As you more critically exercise your natural senses, God will super-sensitize them and add knowledge to make you aware of demonic activity in a person's life. It is not that you are so spiritual that you just stand there, close your eyes and meditate on the Lord, and He speaks a word in your inner ear like, "Sloth." Sometimes that happens. But the usual course of discerning of spirits is that you start in the natural and end up in the supernatural. This also applies in the operation of other gifts of the Holy Spirit.

Prophecy for example—it takes faith to prophesy, and you can prophesy by just starting to speak, and the energizing arrives within it, as God anoints the thought. Speaking in tongues has a faith element and a natural element which, together, God acts upon supernaturally. The gifts that are enumerated in 1 Corinthians 12 have a great deal of the natural involved with the supernatural. Your natural is always in play. That is why others must observe and judge the expression of your gift according to Scripture; sometimes the natural overshadows the spiritual and must be brought back into balance with the Lord's leading.

Once you discern or suspect there is an evil spirit present, begin acting as though there is. God will show you the fact of the matter. Do the right thing by praying and studying the

Bible to show yourself approved unto God. His Word speaks to your spiritual mind.

As you read this book, you should become eager to minister in these aspects of the Word of the Lord. In the course of time, as God leads, become a minister of deliverance just as easily and confidently as you presently minister salvation and healing.

Most believers are not "titled" as ministers but are enabled to perform apostolic feats.

Most believers are not "titled" as ministers but are enabled to perform apostolic feats. This is part of the salvation package and every believer should use the scriptural tools available for defeating our enemy in common.

There are a number of thorny snags that surround the teaching and practice of deliverance. Certainly, I am first to admit no human has all the answers to the invisible world of good and evil. There is more we do not know than we do know.

Satan gains rights and makes claims against Christians through their forbidden violation of divine laws. Even if you were to use a sledgehammer against a demon, if the candidate is committing abominations to the Lord, that spirit will not have to dislodge, and he will tell you so. If the candidate has done something abominable, and has not repented, the demon can withstand your bombardment.

In Matthew 18:20-35 Jesus gives a dissertation on God the Father who shall deliver us to the tormentors—demons—if we hold grudges and resentment in our heart toward anyone. We have to give up the grudges and resentments. We must forgive everyone, except demons whom God also has elected not to forgive.

Jesus went back to His hometown, Nazareth, where Scripture tells us He could not perform many mighty works because of the unbelief of His old acquaintances there (See Matthew 13:58). Unbelief is always a stumbling block and a hindrance to the exercise of spiritual things. Typically, the most distrusting and skeptical people are those who know you intimately. Out-of-towners will believe in you more readily than your family does. The spoof definition of an expert is said to be *anyone from out of town carrying a briefcase*. Deliverance ministers are no exception.

The Lord promises, "Ask, and it shall be given you; seek, and ye shall find; knock, and it shall be opened unto you" Matthew 7:7); and "...whatsoever ye shall ask of the Father in my name, he may give it you" (John 15:16); and "...ye have not because ye ask not" (James 4:2). We must believe this is true. Sometimes our stubborn refusal to believe persists for years before we yield. Ultimately, however, we shall indeed believe the Word of God is true, even if only on judgment day.

To progress from self-examination to ultimate deliverance can be a multi-year process when dealing with a particular torment. I received a physical deliverance in my back after

27 years of waiting, looking, searching, and resisting the devil. After all those years, it came.

DEMONS MADE VISIBLE

There are times when an evil spirit can be "caught on camera". In my case, a demon was seen on an x-ray film of my back taken on a Friday. He is seen rather like a mouse sitting atop my pelvis at the lower lumbar. Prayer on Sunday removed him, as proved by a second x-ray taken the following Monday. I still have both x-ray films to prove it!

In a similar way, there was a middle-age woman in our church in Chicago named Mildred, whom I knew well. Her body remained seriously twisted, even after 32 operations. At one point a demon named Spastic showed up in her x-ray in the form of a black snake wrapped around her spine. This is not a common occurrence, but it sometimes happens that an x-ray will reveal spiritual entities. Often doctors are puzzled by what shows on an x-ray and admit they cannot explain it. In the case of my lower back x-ray, the doctor could not explain the "figure" seen and which he pointed to with four arrows on the negative.

You can receive deliverance in one area of your life and not in another until many years pass. It happened that way for me. After receiving several deliverances, the Lord continued to show me other problem areas in my personality. At first, I did not recognize them as being caused by evil spirits. But after being wakened through years of appropriate knowledge, I was enabled to see their cause.

To undergird the principle that follows, please see confirming scriptures, in this order:1 Corinthians 11:27-31; 2 Corinthians 13:5; 2 Corinthians 12:20-21; and Psalm 26:2. The key to better understanding is to examine oneself in light of Scripture. Do not take the Lord's Supper until you examine yourself. Perhaps the highest expression of *discerning of spirits* is to discern wrong traits, conduct, or spirits within oneself. What is it that is at work within you? It is easy to see and explain the problem of someone else, because his problems are obvious. Right? We look and laugh about it. Not surprisingly they observe us, likewise, laughing as they go!

Yes, discerning evil spirits in someone else is comparatively easy. To discern them within yourself is a different matter. You can bungle your way through life while friends wonder, "Why in the world doesn't he or she get some help? Everybody sees it but you. There is a built-in, self-excusing prejudice that prevents seeing yourself as others see you. Often the remedy may be found through trusted confidants in fellowship.

If you are willing to examine yourself, God is faithful to show you as much as you can bear at one time. He will not put on you more than you can handle. That is why it took me over nine years to unload 23 spirits. Slumber? Yes, I was plagued with Slumber. I have been attacked a number of times when it was perilous to continue driving an automobile. It ought not to have been so because I had had enough rest. Slumber was one of numerous tormenters. Some call him *narcolepsy*.

The Lord has continued to show me spirits that have taken their toll on me, of whom I had been unaware. I just thought it was natural because of the way I had lived before, the circumstances of where I came from, and who I have always been. All of that is true, but my ungodly conduct gave Satan right to invade in the same way the previous 23 came in. I pray, "Lord, show me their names. I will set a time to meet with you and ask others to pray with me. In preparation for that appointed time, I will fast and seek you." A dumb and deaf spirit may not go out upon first command. Jesus said he will be evicted after "prayer and fasting" and by no other way or means (Mark 9:29). After obeying, then command them to go.

Deliverance requires preparation if it is to be thorough and permanent, for it is certain the demon will return and attempt to re-enter. Examining yourself shows the Lord you are willing to get the speck out of your own eye. It demonstrates you are willing to obey His teaching to examine yourself. If you are willing to do it, God is faithful to show you what you do not see.

Read your bible in the knowledge of Hebrews 4:12-13. "For the word of God is quick, and powerful, and sharper than any two-edged sword, piercing even to the dividing asunder of soul and spirit, and of joints and marrow, and is a discerner of the thoughts and intents of the heart. Neither is there any creature that is not manifest in his sight: but all things are naked and opened unto the eyes of him with whom we have to do."

An important technique used in examining yourself is to write brief notes of what you observe in your thoughts and emotions. What we need to do is separate our soul from a spirit. You cannot do it by yourself. You cannot do it just by thinking. Thoughts are too nebulous. You would get so dizzy with the induced whirl of thoughts that you could not concentrate.

Once your observations have been written over months or a year, you will see patterns of thoughts and feelings. Those patterns will help to identify things you think or do that are displeasing to the Lord, even against your will.

A trusted minister might provide a helpful insight. Using our will, we are supposed to be able to do whatever we want to do. If you find that you cannot righteously order your thoughts and actions, you are in bondage. Someone else has taken charge of them — at least in part.

If there is fear of any kind, call it Spirit of Fear, or perhaps specifically Fear of the Future, or of Heights, or Fear of Rejection, etc. Fear usually manifests itself and himself in the same way. Sensual lust usually manifests itself in the same way as Nicotine does. I have never cast out a spirit of Nicotine without also casting out a spirit of Lust with it. Both lurk in bars and nightclubs. Masturbation manifests in the hands exactly like Lust and Nicotine. All may lock your fingers to rigid-stiff when being cast out. These are different spirits having some common characteristics and manifestations when commanded to depart, yet each torment is specialized. The bible says, "fear hath torment". That is exactly what it is. When a person has a spirit of fear, there is inner torment.

My advice to deliverance candidates is to prepare themselves to meet with the Lord, not only by prayer but also with fasting.

The length of a fast could be determined by how much you want deliverance. Should it be two or three meals, three days or a week? One answer is, "What is it worth to you?" I personally want to do everything I know to do and then ask God to perform the miracle which I cannot perform. I suggest fasting at least one full day before the deliverance prayer time. Fasting is making a sacrifice that shows God you really mean business. Also, begin reading the Psalms starting at Psalm 27. Make each one your own prayer to the Lord. Read examples in the New Testament in Matthew, Mark and Luke of the deliverances effected by Jesus Christ in his earthly ministry.

Ask Christians you trust to pray for you. You do not need to reveal confidential matters, except to say you have an appointment with the Lord and that you are earnestly seeking God to grant you the desire of your heart.

Recapping what was shown earlier, spirits are evicted in a variety of ways. There can be coughing, screaming, roaring, and much more. Come to any deliverance service with an open mind so that whichever way God has deliverance for you will not become a stumbling block to you. The task is to get the job done. Standing on formality or etiquette would be a mistake. Come expecting to receive the answer to your prayer.

7

PREPARATION AND DELIVERANCE

AUTHENTIC VS. FAKE MIRACLES

Notable miracles are irrefutable evidence; talk is cheap. The one who has received a miracle comprehends it no matter how uneducated. Witnesses cannot effectively deny them – whether friends, family, neighbors, heathen, religionist, Pharisee, or Christian.

Do not expect deliverance services to be short and do not short cut the presentation of the Word of God just so students can leave early. It is wise to lay the ground rules before the service gets underway. Deliverance services can go long. If someone must leave early, let it be quietly without disturbance.

A deliverance service is for two groups: those who are receiving deliverance from evil spirits, and those who have come to support them in prayer. There should be no uninvolved observers. It is vital that no one foolishly jest or mock God or Satan; to do so would be very dangerous. Evil spirits can leave one person and enter another within two seconds when such a "door" is opened.

GIVING RIGHTS TO SATAN

Committing an act that is hateful or disgusting to the Lord—called "abomination"—opens the way for a demon to enter your personality whether your human spirit is born-again or not. Here we are specifically talking about born-again Christians. Deliverance in the name of the Lord Jesus Christ is usually not available to unbelievers. It is always available to those whose spirit is regenerated—born-again, thereby becoming entitled to all the promises within salvation.

Those who will not acknowledge Jesus Christ cannot receive these benefits. Instead, they remain under the power and bondage of the devil and his tormentors. Satan has power to perform miracles, as seen at Exodus 7:9-12. What we are talking about here is God's deliverance. Satan will sometimes perform a deceptive miracle, sign or wonder for the purpose of increasing one's bondage.

WHAT ARE ABOMINATIONS TO THE LORD?

"Thou shalt have no other gods before me" (Exodus 20:3). As the chief false god, Satan uses his agents to fabricate lesser gods and false religions for your distraction and diversion from the one true God. To wit, committing yourself to religious cults like Buddhism, Confucianism, Taoism, Baha'i Faith, Hinduism, Jainism, Sikhism, Mohammedanism, New Age, and Spiritism; or to organizations and ideologies such as Freemasonry, Communism, Scientology and Dianetics—all of these and others which bypass the Lord Jesus Christ, his virgin birth and atoning blood, lead to demonic bondage.

A Christian's situation is rather like a treasury agent in training. There is no way to know all possible variations in counterfeit currency. What he has to do is to learn everything there is to know about the genuine. Any aspect of a currency bill that is not genuine reveals it is entirely bogus. We likewise must learn what the truth is and then we will know what is false.

Possessing or worshiping idols—graven images—is an abomination to the Lord. See Deuteronomy 7:25-26 and Isaiah 45:16. Do you have any statues or images of false gods in your home? If so, get rid of them now!

If you idolize money, food, a movie star or public figure, you have another god in preference to the One true God.

Sexual sins of every kind are an abomination to the Lord: such as masturbation that becomes bondage, having sex outside the marriage covenant, homosexuality, bestiality, incest, rape, adultery, and more. (See Leviticus 20:10-21 and Deuteronomy 22:5 and 13-30.)

This imperative scripture also admonishes, "The woman shall not wear that which pertaineth unto a man, neither shall a man put on a woman's garment: for all that do so are abomination unto the Lord thy God." Frequently a lady asks, "Does the wearing of slacks or pants by a woman constitute man's clothing? No, not generally, but there are women who wear men's clothing and try to act like a man, even to an extreme. They are usually sexually involved with another woman or sending a strong message that they desire to be thus engaged. Such a woman is called a "butch." There are varying degrees of this. The butch is the aggressive female toward another female. She rejects all the feminine beauty that God gave her and discards female garments to wear men's clothing instead.

She will cut her hair in the fashion of a man's haircut. She might wear a man's leather jacket, pants, and boots. Often you cannot distinguish this person as a woman. She intentionally looks and acts like a man. What she does not know is that a demon has entered to cause, confirm, and make this false personality her permanent bondage. This may appear to be extreme but is more common than most realize.

A garment has no moral value in and of itself and no particular character of its own. At issue is the lust of the flesh to distort what God originally intended. God made women to be obviously feminine and men obviously masculine. They are to be easily distinguishable one from the other.

A woman is not to have sexual relations with a woman, nor a man with another man, as revealed in Romans 1:26-28. For all who do these things, are an abomination to God. Outward expressions reveal intent of the heart. God looks upon the heart. It is only in Christ that we have the power to stand against such inner urges and motivations (See Jeremiah 17:9). God made men and women physically and emotionally different. Each has a defined godly role to play and they are not intended to be mixed. It is Satan who confuses the issue.

Equally unrighteous conduct is that of outright stealing, withholding something from God or man, such as dishonesty in business, owing people money and evading payment, and so much more – all of which gives advantage to the Devil. (Consider Zechariah 5:3; Hosea 4:1-3; Romans 13:9; Ephesians 4:28 and Malachi 3:8-10.)

Proverbs 6 adds "…a proud look; a lying tongue; murder; a heart that devises wicked imaginations; feet that are swift to run to mischief; a false witness; he who sows discord among brethren", resentment and unforgiveness – the holding of a grudge against anyone. Whether someone has wronged you or not is beside the point. Offences must come. To get right with God, you must forgive every person living or dead, before asking the Lord for deliverance. This is a matter between you and God, not the offender.

HOW EVIL SPIRITS GAIN ACCESS TO A CHRISTIAN'S LIFE:

Realize there is no part of the human body or personality that is unavailable for demonic intrusion. These secret agents of Satan probe to find opportunity to invade. Here are just a few circumstances that are opportune for them:

- Evil spirits often invade if you have serious shock or trauma—perhaps an automobile accident, if you have been the victim of a crime, or deeply hurt physically or emotionally.

- The shock of grief experienced when a loved one dies, with mourning and great sorrow taking hold for long periods.
- If you have ever been terribly enraged—it likely gave Satan an opening to enter.
- You went to a horror movie and were filled with exaggerated fear. A spirit named Fear gained opportunity to enter your personality.
- If you have a persistent wrong attitude—Resentment, Pride, Rebellion, Bitterness, or Unforgiveness — persisting in it provides opportunity to the enemy.
- Persistent negative thinking is an open invitation to a demon.
- Immoral, unclean acts: adultery, fornication, lasciviousness, lust, and viewing pornography provide open doors.
- Wrong use of drugs, alcoholic beverages, or nicotine products does too.
- There is the problem of spiritual heredity to the third and fourth generations— (see Exodus 20:5; 34:7; Deuteronomy 5:9). If your parents, grandparents, or other relative from an earlier generation was involved in the occult or committed any other abomination to the Lord, you may have been born with a corresponding evil spirit by inheritance. This is sometimes referred to as "generational iniquity."

Some argue that this is Old Testament legalism. Yes, but Jesus said, "Think not that I am come to destroy the law, or the prophets: I am not come to destroy, but to fulfill" (Matthew 5:17)

"Do we then make void the law through faith? God forbid: yea, we establish the law" (Romans 3:31). And, "…These are the words which I spake unto you, while I was yet with you, that all things must be fulfilled, which were written in the law of Moses, and in the prophets, and in the psalms, concerning me" (Luke 24:44).

Christ fulfilled the law by His perfect life, His redeeming death and resurrection, and by satisfying what the prophets had foretold about the future Savior and Messiah. That body of moral law has not been done away but has been transferred from writing on stones to being written in our heart (See Romans 2:13-15). We are still morally responsible to obey, just as Jesus humbled himself to obey.

INDICATIONS OF DEMON PRESENCE

To be clear, one symptom does not mean that you definitely have an evil spirit active in your life. Usually it requires several tests. The Lord tells us to test or try the spirits to see that they be of God (See 1 John 4:1). A one-time suspicion is not conclusive. I cannot say too strongly, begin taking notes while examining yourself over a course of time. This provides for several tests to confirm your suspicion of evil spirit activity, or otherwise to realize the cause of your problem.

PSYCHOLOGICAL SYMPTOMS

This list is by no means comprehensive but provides an idea of what to look for. These deal primarily with the inward nature and character.

* Evil or destructive emotions or attitudes—persistent or recurrent, which dominate the person from time to time or continually against his own will.

* Resentment: The most common problem we see in deliverance. Oftentimes people have resentments they do not even remember, buried deep within. That is why introspection through self-examination is helpful in determining whether you have an evil spirit problem. You may think, "Well, that's just the way I am, I grew up this way." That may or may not be all there is to it.

The empowering of the gospel of Christ gives you the ability to adjust a negative trait to become positive. Never accept the lie that you cannot change yourself. You can and must become transformed through the power of God. Identify each problem area that does not fulfill the requirements of Scripture. If you are not serious about it, you are not going to receive deliverance. There is no such thing as a small sin that can be excused. Here are additional issues to consider:

- Hatred
- Fear
- Envy

- Insecurity
- Jealousy
- Pride
- Self-pity
- Tension in any form
- Moods with extreme fluctuations

RELIGIOUS SYMPTOMS

- Religious error or bondage—being completely tied to a religious system or fearing to question its leader.
- Submission to unscriptural doctrine and prohibition—if you are doing this now or have been drawn into its snare anytime in your past.
- Shunning, recoiling from, or fighting against the Holy Spirit and His gifts such as speaking in tongues, interpretation of tongues, prophecy, discerning of spirits, working of miracles, etc. – revealed in I Corinthians 12. Demons want to bring us into bondage and error. They do not want us to recognize the truth of God's Word on the matter of receiving the Holy Spirit and doing His works in partnership.
- Unnatural asceticism—extreme self-denial in any category
- Forced celibacy—you believe you have to remain single instead of getting married
- Refusal to eat normal foods

- All forms of superstition—not walking under a ladder (Though common sense applies if someone is on the ladder carrying bricks), not stepping on a crack, wearing some article of clothing to bring luck, nailing a horseshoe above a doorway, keeping a rabbit's foot or using a pendulum for good luck or protection from evil.
- Idolatry
- Resorting to charms, astrology, horoscopes, fortune telling, mediums and clairvoyance.

The Book of Deuteronomy lists more abominations. For example, Deuteronomy 18 lists occult sins including, but not limited to: human sacrifice, divination, fortune telling; necromancy (an effort to call up the dead); horoscope, Ouija board, astrology, consulting a witch, a charmer, an enchanter, a medium, wizard, psychic, attending a séance, witchcraft, magician/magic, sorcery, tarot card reading, trying to influence another by drugs, charms, earrings, bracelets, amulets, pronouncing curses and the like. Abortion also is the equivalent of sacrificing a child to a pagan god like Molech or Baal. Abortion is as abominable as any other premeditated murder (See Revelation 21:8).

If you have ever participated in any of the above for any reason, you have thereby given a demon the right to enter into you. It does not necessarily mean that he did, but if not, he missed his opportunity. Never forget that Satan is a legalist! He will hold you to every agreement with him, by word or deed, whether you were knowledgeable, remembered, or have forgotten it!

ENSLAVING HABITS:

- Gluttony, essentially of food but may include binging on television or social media
- Alcohol
- Nicotine
- Drugs—prescription or street
- Sexual Immorality
- Sexual Perversion—without exception, every kind of sexual perversion is demonic.
- Uncontrollable unclean thoughts, fantasies or looks with your eyes
- Blasphemy, Mockery, and Foul Language

PHYSICAL SYMPTOMS:

- Unnatural restlessness or talkativeness
- Sighing and muttering—either one or both
- Frothing at the mouth
- Foul breath
- Body stench you cannot wash away
- Fast palpitations of the heart
- Insanity

The following can be, but are not necessarily demonic:

- Insomnia
- Seizures and convulsions
- Muscle cramps
- Epilepsy I would say is nearly always demonic
- Migraine headache
- Sinus infection
- Tumors and ulcers
- Heart disease
- Arthritis—I would always treat as a demon first, although arthritis may also develop from a natural cause.
- Paralysis
- Muteness
- Deafness
- Blindness

Demons delight in tormenting. However, it is not always the devil who delivers you to demon bondage. Sometimes it is God. (See 1 Samuel 16:14-15 and Matthew 18:34-35). The tormentors are demons who are invoked because of one's unforgiveness. We make the choice to obey the Holy Spirit or to remain in bondage. This is true of every Christian.

8

DELIVERANCE PROCESS AND EXAMPLES

KNOW YOUR AUTHORITY

About one fourth of Jesus' public miracles were the casting out of evil spirits one-on-one. Let us look at what the Bible teaches us: Know Your Authority.

Deliverance from a legion of demons is not an ordinary miracle. Some miracles in Scripture are notable but not called "great things." Demonic deliverance is special, called by the Lord "great things". While every intervention of God is miraculous, most are not described as "special miracles". Unlike demons, physical sickness and disease are visible, cannot hide, have no intelligence of their own, do not resist or willfully torment us.

The facts of demons are different. In addition to being invisible, they are persons with intelligence, cannot be killed, never die, are permanently evil beyond choice. They are a perpetual threat under orders to steal, kill, and destroy us. A demon who caused a cancer to develop will return to inflame it repeatedly after its remission was obtained. They hide to conceal themselves from discovery in the human body.

A specific deliverance from a demonic invasion was not categorized as sickness or disease. Jesus instructed a man he had delivered from hopeless bondage to a legion of demons in Mark 5:19, "Go home to thy friends, and tell them how great things the Lord hath done for thee." The account in Luke 8:39 adds, "and he went his way and published throughout the whole city how great things Jesus had done unto him."

Mark 6:7 says, "And he called unto him the twelve, and began to send them forth by two and two; and gave them [and us by extension] power over unclean spirits." This assignment of power has never been repealed. It is as viable today as when the Lord gave it.

In Matthew 10:7-8 Jesus says, "And as ye go, preach, saying, the kingdom of heaven is at hand. Heal the sick, cleanse the lepers, raise the dead, cast out devils: freely ye have received, freely give." "Freely" means there should be no asking for money. The Lord supplies our needs.

Luke 10:17-20, "And the seventy returned again with joy, saying, Lord, even the devils are subject unto us through thy name. And he said unto them, I beheld Satan as lightning fall from heaven. Behold, I give unto you power to tread on serpents and scorpions [types of demons], and over all the power of the enemy: and nothing shall by any means hurt you. Notwithstanding in this rejoice not, that the spirits are subject unto you; but rather rejoice, because your names are written in heaven." Again, "the spirits are subject unto you…". It is a joyous fact that we have power over evil spirits in Jesus' name. That is our privilege in salvation. Wonderful as that is, Jesus is saying to us, "Rejoice not that the spirits are subject unto you, but rather rejoice because your names are written in heaven." This is primary over other gifts and power granted to believers.

No single demon can match the power or totally control the superior personality of a human.

Nevertheless, He is saying in the same text, "I give unto you authority to tread on serpents and scorpions, and over all the power of the enemy." Who is the enemy? It is Satan and his legions of demons at all levels. More often than not you will deal with the lesser demons. Once in a while you may run into a principality-level demon—a prince—and you will know when it happens. He might wrestle you all over the room, light it up in brilliant light, or both.

1 John 3:8 b says this, "…For this purpose the Son of God was manifested, that he might destroy the works of the devil." Jesus came to destroy the works of the devil. What is the devil's works? They are the torments, sickness, infirmities, and bondages placed upon us by demons. In John 5:15 Jesus says, "…*without me* ye can do nothing." But *without us* Jesus will do nothing more. Also, "As my Father hath sent me, even so send I you [for the same purpose]" (John 20:21). Our job, yours and mine, is to destroy the works of the devil wherever we go. That is what this book is about!

In Revelation 12:10-11 God says, "...for the accuser of our brethren is cast down, which accused them before our God day and night. And they [the saints] overcame him [Satan] by the blood of the Lamb, and by the word of their testimony; and they loved not their lives unto the death."

Both Jesus and Satan have authority, though the Lord's is supreme. Matthew 12:22-28: "Then was brought unto him one possessed with a devil, blind, and dumb: and he healed him, insomuch that the blind and dumb both spake and saw. And all the people were amazed, and said, Is not this the son of David? But when the Pharisees heard it, they said, this fellow doth not cast out devils, but by Beelzebub the prince of the devils. And Jesus knew their thoughts, and said unto them, every kingdom divided against itself is brought to desolation; and every city or house divided against itself shall not stand: And if Satan cast out Satan, he is divided against himself; how shall then his kingdom stand? And if I by [another name for Satan] Beelzebub cast out devils, by whom do your children cast them out? Therefore, they shall be your judges. But if I cast out devils by the Spirit of God, then the kingdom of God is come unto you." Certain followers of the Pharisees attempted to cast out demons. No further details are given. It is probable that all their attempts failed, as was the case for Sceva's seven sons in Acts 19:13-17, reported above.

Mark 1:23-28, "And there was in their synagogue a man with an unclean spirit; and he cried out, saying, let us alone; what have we to do with thee, thou Jesus of Nazareth? Art, thou come to destroy us? I know thee who thou art, the Holy

One of God. And Jesus rebuked him, saying, hold thy peace, and come out of him. When the unclean spirit had torn him, and cried with a loud voice, he came out of him.

Notice that Jesus rebuked the spirit saying, "Hold your peace and come out of him!" What did the spirit do? The spirit tore the man and cried with a loud voice…". The spirit did not hold his peace as Jesus commanded him. Instead, he expressed his violence and yelled loudly. It was after doing so that he came out of him.

"And they were all amazed, insomuch that they questioned among themselves, saying, What thing is this? What new doctrine is this? for with authority commandeth he even the unclean spirits, and they do obey him. And immediately his fame spread abroad throughout all the region round about Galilee." Fame can be negative and costly or positive and helpful, and likely will be both for the practitioner of deliverance.

Jesus did not make the demons behave. His reasons remain private to Himself (See Mark 9:17-29). He had the power to cast them out and that is what He did. But they did not behave. Many screamed, roared, foamed at the mouth, tore the victims, harmed and hurt them. This does not mean it will always happen. The point is, in the scriptural examples of deliverance by Jesus Christ, these things happened. You and I cannot expect something different from what God's Word plainly tells us occurs, because those cases were provided for our learning. We are to expect, prepare, and be ready for them to happen. We must accept the facts of the bible. It is the way of deliverance. Sometimes they obey when we command them to shut their mouth, but not always. They are not going to behave or become gentle. They did not do so for Jesus or the apostles, and they do not behave for today's disciples.

Mark 7:25-30 says, "For a certain woman, whose young daughter had an unclean spirit, heard of him, and came and fell at his feet [She was not proud. She had a problem. Her daughter had an unclean spirit and needed help.]: the woman was Greek, a Syrophenician by nation, and she besought him that he would cast forth the devil out of her daughter. But Jesus said unto her, Let the children (Jews) first be filled: for it is not meet to take the children's bread, and to cast it unto the dogs. And she answered and said unto him, Yes, Lord: yet the dogs under the table eat of the children's crumbs. And he said unto her, for this saying go thy way; the devil is gone out of thy daughter. And when she was come to her house, she found the devil gone out, and her daughter laid upon the bed." Jews often referred to pagan Gentiles as dogs in those days.

Jesus does what He says He will do, then and now, whether for Jew or Gentile. Faith is always honored. Luke 9:38-43, "And, behold, a man of the company cried out, saying, Master, I beseech thee, look upon my son for he is mine only child. And lo, a spirit taketh him, and he suddenly crieth out; and it teareth him that he foameth again and bruising him hardly departeth from him. And I besought thy disciples to cast him out; and they could not. And Jesus answering said, O faithless and perverse generation, how long shall I be with you, and suffer you? Bring thy son hither. And as he was yet a coming, the devil threw him down and tare him. And Jesus rebuked the unclean spirit, and healed the child, and delivered him again to his father. And they were all amazed at the mighty power of God."

I want you to comprehend how God sees our deliverance from the bondage of a demon. Here he describes the witnessing crowd's typical reaction: *"they were all amazed at the mighty power of God."* This is not the common vernacular of Scripture. The Lord is making a point! When God brings deliverance from demonic bondage here or elsewhere, he describes it as the *"... great and mighty things God has done and the mighty power of God."* Let every believer and Christian leader acknowledge it. Moreover, learn to overtly and publicly perform the same miracles, which is our privilege!

SPEAKING THE WORD

"The word of God is quick, and powerful, and sharper than any two-edged sword, piercing even to the dividing asunder of soul and spirit, and of the joints and marrow, and is a discerner of the thoughts and intents of the heart" (Hebrews 4:12). The word of God works as a sword and sledgehammer. Remember that evil spirits are not things. They are *persons* of a depraved society in which few are powerful and intellectual, and many are stupid. That fact mirrors human society in which everyone must die because of sin. They hear, see, talk, and feel. It is important to present the Word of God during deliverance because they know it is true. Romans 10:7 tells us that faith comes by hearing the Word of God. When we, and demons, hear the Word of God, we are built up in our faith to the same degree the demonic stronghold is torn down by it.

Speaking the Word of God is the weapon in our warfare that weakens them for the overwhelming invasion of the Spirit of God. Mark 3:11-15, "And unclean spirits, when they saw him, fell down before him, and cried, saying, Thou art the Son of God. And he straightly charged them that they should not make him known. *They knew who he was. And when we declare this same fact to a demon, he still knows who Jesus is!*

And he (Jesus) goeth up into a mountain, and calleth unto him whom he would [not everyone]: and they came unto him. And he ordained twelve, that they should be with him, and that he might send them [*and us*] forth to preach, and to have power to heal sicknesses, and to cast out devils..."

FORGIVENESS

Matthew 6:12-14 "...forgive us our debts as we forgive our debtors. And lead us not into temptation but deliver us from evil [literally: the evil one]: For thine is the kingdom, and the power, and the glory, forever. Amen. For if ye forgive men their trespasses, your heavenly Father will also forgive you." Note that last sentence: If you forgive... That is on the positive side. Let's look at the negative side in the next verse:

Matthew 6:15 says, "But if ye forgive not men their trespasses, neither will your Father forgive your trespasses."

In order to be forgiven of your sins and trespasses, it is required that you forgive others. Which others? All others! Only the living ones? No. All offenders—even if they have died. Why is it important to forgive someone even after they have died? Because your forgiveness is between you and God, not you and the offender. Forgiving everyone clears the channel between you and God, not you and the forgiven person. The offender is simply the *object* of your forgiveness. But the problem was between you and God, not you and that person. You must forgive.

See also Matthew 18:21-35 and Mark 11:25-26. These passages provide a vital lesson. Jesus emphasizes it in a parable: "Then came Peter to him, and said, Lord, how oft shall my brother sin against me, and I forgive him? till seven times? Jesus saith unto him, I say not unto thee, until seven times: but, until seventy times seven [490 times, which is essentially without limit].

Therefore, is the kingdom of heaven likened unto a certain king, which would take account of his servants. And when he had begun to reckon, one was brought unto him, which owed him ten thousand talents [*equivalent of six million dollars*]. But forasmuch as he had not to pay, his lord commanded him to be sold, and his wife, and children, and all that he had, and payment to be made. The servant therefore fell down, and worshipped him, saying, Lord, have patience with me, and I will pay thee all. Then the lord of that servant was moved with compassion, and loosed him, and forgave him the debt. But the same servant went out, and found one of his fellow servants, which owed him a hundred pence [*about eighteen dollars*]: and he laid hands on him, and took him by the throat, saying, Pay me that thou owest. And his fellow servant fell down at his feet, and besought him, saying, have patience with me, and I will pay thee all. And he would not: but went and cast him into prison, till he should pay the debt. So, when his fellow servants saw what was done, they were very sorry, and came and told unto their lord all that was done. Then his lord, after that he had called him, said unto him, O thou wicked servant, I forgave thee all that debt, because thou desiredst me: Shouldest not thou also have had compassion on thy fellow servant, even as I had pity on thee? And his lord was wroth, and delivered him to the tormentors, till he should pay all that was due unto him. So likewise, shall my heavenly Father do also unto you, if ye from your hearts forgive not everyone his brother their trespasses."

It is important to understand that it is God the Father in heaven who will deliver you and me to the tormentors if we fail to forgive anyone. We must forgive. It is not Satan who will deliver you to the demon tormentors. It is God the Father.

Mark 11:25-26, "And when ye stand praying, forgive, if ye have ought against any: that your Father also which is in heaven may forgive you your trespasses. But if ye do not forgive, neither will your Father which is in heaven forgive your trespasses." Realize that if God does not forgive your trespasses, you can never enter into heaven. Quite to the opposite you will be cast into hell forever. How important is that, compared to you holding a grudge against someone?

DELIVERANCE PROCESS AND EXAMPLES

ASK, SEEK, KNOCK

Matthew 7:7-11 says, "Ask, and it shall be given you; seek, and ye shall find; knock, and it shall be opened unto you: For everyone that asketh, receiveth; and he that seeketh, findeth; and to him that knocketh, it shall be opened. Or what man is there of you, whom if his son ask bread, will he give him a stone? Or if he asks a fish, will he give him a serpent? If ye then, being evil, know how to give good gifts unto your children, how much more shall your Father which is in heaven give good things to them that ask him?"

We are talking about asking God for deliverance from the torment and bondage of demons. God says He is going to deliver you if you ask Him - provided you meet His conditions. Ask according to the will of God, including forgiveness of all others, and you shall have it!

PRAYER AND FASTING

Matthew 17:14-21, "And when they were come to the multitude, there came to him a certain man, kneeling down to him, and saying, Lord, have mercy on my son: for he is lunatic, and sore vexed: for oft times he falleth into the fire, and oft into the water. And I brought him to thy disciples, and they could not cure him. Then Jesus answered and said, O faithless and perverse generation, how long shall I be with you? How long shall I suffer you? Bring him hither to me. And Jesus rebuked the devil; and he departed out of him: and the child was cured from that very hour."

It is noteworthy that the time frame in which the demon departed, and the child thereby cured is said to be "that very hour". This indicates it was not "immediate." This is often the case. Many times, the cure may occur within two weeks or longer. In Ephesians 6, the Lord tells us through Apostle Paul that we "…wrestle against principalities and powers". Deliverance does not usually culminate within a moment. It is a wrestling match – not a single knockout punch – and often can require hours of battle on the imperfect human level to attain a major deliverance.

Verse 19: "Then came the disciples to Jesus apart, and said, "Why could not we cast him out?" And Jesus said unto them, "Because of your unbelief: for verily I say unto you, if ye have faith as a grain of mustard seed, ye shall say unto this mountain, remove hence to yonder place; and it shall remove; and nothing shall be impossible unto you. Howbeit this kind [referring only to a *demonic* mountain] goeth not out but by prayer and fasting. Jesus' words here are why I say you should pray with fasting on behalf of your own deliverance, and for that of others. It is another aspect of fervent prayer that avails much, saving time and frustration, and proves the seeker's determination and tenacity to win the battle.

Mark 9:17-29, "And one of the multitude answered and said, Master, I have brought unto thee my son, which hath a dumb spirit [preventing speech]; And wheresoever he taketh him, he teareth him: and he foameth, and gnasheth with his teeth, and pineth away: and I spake to thy disciples that they should cast him out; and they could not. He answereth him, and saith, O faithless generation, how long shall I be with you? How long shall I suffer you? Bring him unto me. And they brought him unto him: and when he saw him, straightway the spirit tare him; and he fell on the ground, and wallowed foaming. And he (Jesus) asked his father, how long is it ago since this came unto him? And he said, of a child. And oft times it hath cast him into the fire, and into the waters, to destroy him: but if thou canst do anything, have compassion on us, and help us. Jesus said unto him, if thou canst believe, all things are possible to him that believeth. And straightway the father of the child cried out, and said with tears, Lord, I believe; help thou mine unbelief. When Jesus saw that the people came running together, he rebuked the foul spirit, saying unto him, thou dumb and deaf spirit, I charge thee, come out of him, and enter no more into him. And the spirit cried, and rent him sore, and came out of him: and he was as one dead; insomuch that many said, He is dead. But Jesus took him by the hand and lifted him up; and he arose. And when he was come into the house, his disciples asked him privately, why could not we cast him out? And he said unto them, this kind can come forth by nothing, but by prayer and fasting."

Here we are told that a violent "dumb and deaf" spirit requires fasting with prayer before he can be evicted. Without fasting, the effort is futile.

CONFESS AND REPENT

1 John 1:8-9: "If we say that we have no sin, we deceive ourselves, and the truth is not in us. If we confess our sins, he is faithful and just to forgive us our sins, and to cleanse us from all unrighteousness." We must not deny that we have sin. We must say what the Bible says—that we do have sin. We must confess our sins, and only then does God forgive and cleanse us from all unrighteousness. With the heart man believes but believing alone does not constitute salvation.

With the mouth confession is made unto salvation. You are not saved until you truthfully confess it with your mouth. Tell others what God has done for you. Bring glory to God. This fact is confirmed in Romans 10:9-10: "That if thou shalt confess with thy mouth the Lord Jesus, and shalt believe in thine heart that God hath raised him from the dead, thou shalt be saved. For with the heart man believeth unto righteousness, and with the mouth confession is made unto salvation."

DISCERNING THE SPIRITS

Matthew 8:16-17 says, "When the even was come, they brought unto him many that were possessed with devils: and he cast out the spirits with his word, and healed all that were sick: That it might be fulfilled which was spoken by Esaias the prophet, saying, Himself [Jesus] took our infirmities, and bare our sicknesses." The spirits and condition of sickness spoken of in verse 16 relate to all types of infirmities— spiritual, mental, or physical, including demonically induced deformity, sickness, and disease. In the original manuscript Isaiah 53:4-5 includes "pain" among the sin penalties that Jesus paid on our behalf.

Matthew 9:32-33 says, "As they went out, behold, they brought to him a dumb man possessed with a devil. And when the devil was cast out, the dumb spake: and the multitudes marveled, saying, it was never so seen in Israel."

Mark 1:32-34: "And at even, when the sun did set, they brought unto him [Jesus] all that were diseased, and them that were possessed with devils. [*Note the two classifications: some were diseased, and others possessed with demons. Some likely were both diseased and possessed.*] And all the city was gathered together at the door. And he healed many that were sick of divers diseases, [Note that they brought all that were diseased and he healed many. It does not say he healed all.] and cast out many devils; [He cast out many, but not all demons.] and suffered not the devils to speak, because they knew him. The Lord has all the options, while ours are limited by ignorance, unbelief, or fear.

Mark 5:1-20, "And they came over unto the other side of the sea, into the country of the Gadarenes, And when he was come out of the ship, immediately there met him out of the tombs a man with an unclean spirit, Who had his dwelling among the tombs; and no man could bind him, no, not with chains: Because that he had been often bound with fetters and chains, and the chains had been plucked asunder by him, and the fetters broken in pieces: neither could any man tame him. And always, night and day, he was in the mountains, and in the tombs, crying, and cutting himself with stones [cutting yourself is demon-inspired]. But when he saw Jesus afar off, he ran and worshiped him, and cried with a loud voice, and said, what have I to do with thee, Jesus, thou Son of the most high God? I adjure thee by God, that thou torment me not. For he said unto him, Come out of the man, thou unclean spirit. And he [Jesus] asked him, what is thy name? [This is the only place in Scripture where Jesus asks a demon his name.] And he answered, saying, my name is Legion: for we are many. And he besought him much that he would not send them away out of the country. Now there was there nigh unto the mountains a great herd of swine feeding. And all the devils besought him, saying, send us into the swine, that we may enter them. And forthwith Jesus gave them leave. And the unclean spirits went out and entered into the swine: and the herd ran violently down a steep place into the sea, (they were about two thousand;) and were choked in the sea."

The 2,000 pigs died, but the demons did not die. Those very same ones continue to harass, torment, invade, and put men and women in bondage in our society. Among their indiscriminate victims are prisoners, politicians, preachers, and ordinary folk like us.

"...And they that fed the swine fled, and told it in the city, and in the country. And they went out to see what it was that was done. And they come to Jesus, and see him that was possessed with the devil, and had the legion, sitting, and clothed, and in his right mind: and they were afraid. And they that saw it told them how it befell to him that was possessed with the devil, and also concerning the swine. And they began to pray him to depart out of their coasts. And when he was come into the ship, he that had been possessed with the devil prayed him that he might be with him. Howbeit Jesus suffered him not, but saith unto him, go home to thy friends, and tell them how great things the Lord hath done for thee, and hath had compassion on thee. And he departed and began to publish in Decapolis how great things Jesus had done for him: and all men did marvel." You can read more details of this account in Luke 8:26-39.

I call attention to certain features of this man's bondage that are widespread in the Christian Church at large. Admittedly the case at hand is one of the most terrible. The details given, however, are for the purpose of comparison to our own, and are not to be ignored only because they describe unusual ferocity.

The Lord here shows us the reality, depth, and scope of the warfare in which we are engaged, though few are willing to acknowledge it.

Notice the all-comprehensive bondage demons may put one under, and the supernatural power they exhibit through a man they inhabit, strong enough to repeatedly break iron chains and shackles; the fearsomeness of his character; his demeanor; and habitation among the tombs and in the wilderness, and in the mountains. Humans could not bind or restrain him. He was caused to mutilate himself with sharp stones—a wild man indeed, who ripped off his clothing to remain naked.

We are shown the incredible power of the human personality—though being in pain, agony, and misery, he was still able to avoid death long enough to await deliverance by One stronger than the Legion of demons – numbered in thousands.

As powerful as Legion was however, "…when he saw Jesus afar off, he ran and worshiped him…" [Mark 5:6] begging not to be tormented or commanded to "go out into the deep" (Luke 8:31). Jesus could have sent them deep into hell but that was to await another time. Instead, He consented to their request to enter into "unclean" beasts—a large herd of swine. Thus, they fled and destroyed the swine through drowning.

The victim thereby was wonderfully set free, fully clothed himself, and was restored to his right mind. A salient point is that, "…the whole multitude of the country of the Gadarenes round about besought him [Jesus] to depart from them; for they were taken with great fear…" (Luke 8:37)

Fear is both an emotion and the name and character of an evil spirit (See 2 Timothy 1:7). These Gadarenes were not the only ones who express fear. The Christian Church at large is also fearful. Teachers, pastors, and denomination leaders have fled wholesale from this truth of Jesus. Effectively they have "besought him to depart from them: and have driven Him away from their coast. This "driving away" tactic extends not only to the deliverance work done by Jesus then, but also to the

DELIVERANCE PROCESS AND EXAMPLES

few modern disciples who dare cast demons out of Christian victims today. Think it through.

When Jesus expresses such compassion as to deliver you from terrible bondage of demons, be sure to tell your friends the great thing the Lord has done for you! Do not be shy about it. Be bold! Give honor to God who desires glory, pleasure, recognition, and fellowship. He is saying, if you want to retain deliverance from the demonic bondage of addictions and behavior beyond your control, be willing to testify to somebody! Do not be ashamed about it. Otherwise He will be ashamed of you on judgment day. (See Mark 8:38 and Luke 9:26.)

Luke 13:11-13: "And, behold, there was a woman which had a spirit of infirmity eighteen years, and was bowed together, and could in no wise lift up herself. And when Jesus saw her, he called her to him and said unto her, Woman, thou art loosed from thine infirmity. And he laid his hands on her: and immediately she was made straight, and glorified God." Notice that the infirmity was not an organically defective body, but a spirit inside who manifested in her body. This is often the case. A condition that seems altogether physical may be purely spiritual and can be chased away. In this case, Jesus placed both hands on her to impart the substance of faith against the demon for deliverance.

BIND AND LOOSE

Matthew 18:18-20 says, "Verily I say unto you, Whatsoever ye shall bind on earth shall be bound in heaven: and whatsoever ye shall loose on earth shall be loosed in heaven. Again, I say unto you, that if two of you shall agree on earth as touching anything that they shall ask, it shall be done for them of my Father which is in heaven. For where two or three are gathered together in my name, there am I in the midst of them." The principle is that two or more comprise greater force than one alone, the Spirit of God being active. Arbitrary spirit-binding or loosing is not a human prerogative until first authorized in heaven. Be sure in your spirit that you are not presuming to have authority that you have not proved.

Matthew 12:43-45: "When the unclean spirit is gone out of a man, he walketh through dry places, seeking rest, and findeth none. Then he saith, I will return into my house from whence I came out; and when he is come, he findeth it empty, swept, and garnished [furnished]. Then goeth he, and taketh with himself seven other spirits more wicked than himself, and they enter in and dwell there: and the last state of that man is worse than the first. [It is better that a man not be delivered if he is going to leave his house empty.] Even so shall it be also unto this wicked generation." This is important. A demonic spirit has no rest outside a body—preferring a human body. Notice the demon is calling the human body, "my house." Jesus is telling us there is nothing wrong with having your house clean and furnished, but it must not remain empty. You must ask the Lord to fill the empty places with the Holy Spirit when an evil spirit has been forcibly evicted.

Luke 11:24-26 presents the same account as in Matthew 12:43-45. "When the unclean spirit is gone out of a man, he walketh through dry places, seeking rest; and finding none, he saith, I will return unto my house whence I came out. And when he cometh, he findeth it swept and garnished. Then goeth he, and taketh to him seven other spirits more wicked than himself; and they enter in, and dwell there: and the last state of that man is worse than the first." The Lord determined that this point was significant enough to repeat for emphasis, knowing it would generally be shunned.

9

WHAT TO EXPECT AND HOW TO RECEIVE YOUR DELIVERANCE

An occasional outburst of frustration does not define your character. Neither does it prove that an evil spirit has spoken or invaded.

Wanting to evict an undesirable "tenant" does not generally constitute an emergency. He has most likely occupied his room with impunity as though he had a long-term lease. There is a proper and orderly course to be followed, just as in evicting a rental tenant who has occupied your house either as a squatter having no right to be there, or as an undesirable tenant under contract.

What is true in the natural is true in the spiritual. A candidate seeking deliverance should not expect complete restoration within an hour or a month. A deliverance miracle after repentance begins a restorative process over time.

You have seen from Scripture that demons talk and that they have a certain dominion of power. They make noise—sometimes crying in a loud voice in mortal pain, sometimes admitting they are engulfed in flames, screaming, "Move your hand, you're killing me!" As the evil spirit moves, our hand moves parallel as though pushing them. Sometimes evil spirits try to tear the individual, most times they do not. Sometimes they cause foaming at the mouth of the person they inhabit, most times they don't. All the diverse deliverance manifestations that occurred when Jesus ministered them also occur today. Sadly, few teach it that way and almost none demonstrate it, which essentially proves their rejection of its validity.

There are aspects of deliverance we might call mechanical. Knowing them will enable you to better facilitate ministry to others. No one is totally exempt from an evil spirit's influence, including clergy in general, and other ministers of deliverance, whether they are born again, baptized in the Holy Spirit, speak in tongues, and cast out demons. Valid religious acts do not prove you are demon-free. Religious spirits operate incessantly.

Valid religious acts do not prove you are demon-free.

During deliverance, no one should lay hands on the candidate unless it is requested by the lead minister. The laying on of hands is not a mere performance, ritual, or obedience within a doctrine. Rather it is for imparting spiritual substance. What is imparted can only be what the hand-layer has in or upon himself. We impart the *substance of faith* into the person, and in a deliverance context that impartation is against the demon who does not belong there. The caution of Scripture is, "…know them which labour among you…" (1Thessalonians 5:12). It would be improper and dangerous to allow a stranger or immature believer to impart something upon you.

Demonic manifestations are numerous and varied. Do not become alarmed at the uncommon. Not everyone will receive deliverance. Remember, Jesus did not cast spirits out of everyone who had demons in them. He knows and ministers to those whom he has called to be his family (See John 15:16; Acts 2:39; and Romans 8:28-30). He further asserted, "…ye must be born again" (John 3:7).

The word spirit is *pneuma* in Greek. Whether it is holy or evil, the consistency of spirit is defined as air, wind, or breath. It takes an undetermined amount of "empty" space for a spirit to fit within. There is more space in the mid-section of the physical body than in the throat area. Demons can dwell in what Scripture refers to as the bowel (torso)—also considered to be the resident place of the Holy Spirit and the human spirit. There is a lot of space in this section of the body, as compared to the narrow channel of the throat. When a spirit begins to move, he usually moves up through the respiratory system, into the throat, and then out of the mouth or nose.

From the outside we exert spiritual influence to cause that spirit to begin to move from his dwelling place into upper areas of the body. As the minister dislodges the spirit by impartation and prayer, you – the deliverance candidate - should begin expelling breath in an effort to get that spirit caught up in the outgoing blast of air.

When the little pocket of air gets up into your throat, most times there is a retching or catching in your throat so that you feel a need to cough. There can be a belch or a long sigh. There can be a shriek, scream, or crying. Often there is little reaction, and sometimes much. The point is, when deliverance is available, you should not be so shy, polite and courteous that you suppress it. Do not be ashamed if you need to burp, belch, cough, or scream. If you begin to have a quivering deep inside, or a tenseness in your back, let it happen, help it leave. Whatever your body feels like doing at the time, let your body do it openly, freely, expressively, exuberantly, with zeal, because that is what you are looking for! If you want deliverance, receive it as the Lord demonstrated it, in Jesus' name!

In the case of coughing, you can expect a certain amount of phlegm—I call that a habitation of the devil. All demons are unclean. They are the vilest, dirtiest creatures you can imagine. They love uncleanness, and quite frankly, demons stink. For that matter, there is nothing inside the human body that smells good. Let us be frank; any outward expression of anything inside the body is always accompanied by stench.

PRACTICAL PREPARATIONS

It is helpful to have a box of tissues ready for use when you feel like coughing or spitting. Do not press a tissue up to your mouth to suppress as usual. You want to keep that channel as open as possible. Not only is the demon being compressed in your throat, he tries to make a U-turn! He is trying to hang on with everything he has. Keep the exit open. If vomiting seems imminent, prepare for it by arranging for a wastebasket to be nearby. These are practical, common sense measures.

In conclusion, I will lead you in a prayer that ensures you are salvation-qualified, as you seek the Lord Jesus Christ for your deliverance miracle. James 4:7 says, "Submit yourselves therefore to God. Resist the devil, and he will flee from you." The first part of the prayer will be submitting yourself to God according to the Scriptures, acknowledging that Jesus Christ is the name of the Lord; that He came to earth in the form of a man; died on the cross for your sins; descended into hell, taking from Satan the keys of hell and death; preached to the spirits in prison; arose from the dead on the third day; and ascended back to God the Father in heaven, where He now intercedes on your behalf. Then you will thank Him as you receive His forgiveness. From Scripture you know He requires that you forgive all others. You will say to God that you do forgive all others, living or dead—and you must forgive. It is not only the words that make the difference. You must speak out of the depth of your heart. This is not about how you feel about the person who hurt you. God is interested in your decision to forgive them. If God truly has your will, that is enough for now. Just say, "Lord, in spite of my contrary feelings, I have decided to forgive them for every evil word and deed, just as fully as I ask your forgiveness." You will receive only as much forgiveness from God as you give to others. Do not make any vow to God that you are not going to keep. In Ecclesiastes 5:4-5 we are warned not to make a vow and not keep it.

WHAT TO EXPECT AND HOW TO RECEIVE DELIVERANCE

The first condition of deliverance is humility. You must come to Jesus. You must not be ashamed to ask the Lord Jesus Christ for deliverance. Confess that you want him to deliver you from demon bondage. You must be honest. A public confession of particular sins is not necessary, but as you ask God to forgive you, you must internally acknowledge and forsake all of your sins—especially the ones that flash before your mind. Confess them to the Lord. Other people do not have to hear all your words, although sometimes it is important for another person to hear a particular confession for a special reason. That is not always the case.

Renounce and disavow all known sins. Do you remember the three times Peter denied Jesus Christ before the cock crowed? Later, Jesus made Peter confess Him three times—one for each denial, because that balanced the legal transaction equally. If you have pornographic literature or movies in your house, get rid of it all. Burn it. Block such sites from your computer, television, and iPhone. If you have idols or images of pagan gods in your house, get rid of them. Otherwise their demons do not have to depart. If all this is circumstantially impossible at the moment, the Lord will accept your commitment to do so at your earliest opportunity. God will honor it. Again, do not fail to honor your commitment to God.

Matthew 18:18 states that we have the power and ability in Christ to break a bondage. Wherever it applies in your life, loose yourself from the dominion of mother, father, grandmother, boss, friend, anyone in the family that has been involved in the occult—loose yourself in Jesus' name from any and all bondage exercised over you.

Try to pinpoint the time and place when a spirit would have gained a right to enter into you. Identify the source and renounce it in the presence of others. As in a legal court of law where witnesses are required, in deliverance you also stand in a spiritual courtroom. Satan is the Prosecutor accusing the brethren. Jesus Christ is your advocate—your Defense Attorney. God is the Judge, while we and holy angels are witnesses.

Demons and holy angels listen to hear your words, which determine what they do next.

Demons and holy angels listen to hear your words, which determine what they do next. Declare aloud that you hereby break every curse passed to you from the iniquities of all previous generations of family heritage.

Offensively, deliverance is the time for you to attack. You have been defensive long enough. It is a solemn time, a serious time. There has already been war in the heavenlies on your behalf, and it culminates here as you seriously engage in battle with determination to be victorious.

MINISTER'S PRAYER

Minister: Father, I come to you in Jesus' name. Your Word tells us that apart from Jesus, man can do nothing. Lord, we implore you to bring your delivering Spirit that your people might be set free. I declare that the blood of Jesus Christ covers every family represented here, all the children, all the possessions—the things over which You have given us stewardship—we claim the merit and power of the blood of Jesus.

Lord, we ask you to loose angels to war in the heavenlies and to minister to your saints. Place guards over their houses, lands, properties, and vehicles of your people. Praise the name of the Lord. Forgive us all our sins, Lord God.

Let the power of our Lord be great. Holy Spirit attend us now, in the mighty name of Jesus!

Minister's preliminary instruction: You can expect manifestations moments after you have prayed this prayer as led by me. When I tell you to expel those spirits, I want you to begin to strongly expel air from deep down, expecting the evil spirits to vacate. Your task is to cooperate with the Holy Spirit—the Lord says, "quench not the Spirit!" This is your personal prayer to Almighty God against pathetic quivering demons!

WHAT TO EXPECT AND HOW TO RECEIVE YOUR DELIVERANCE

CANDIDATE'S PRAYER

(PRAYER WARRIORS: Right here is where you begin to pray for those seeking deliverance, making confessions while reading this book.)

Repeat after me now:

Lord Jesus Christ,
> I do believe you are the Son of God.
> I believe you came to earth in the form of a man, that you died on the cross for my sins, descended into hell, taking the keys of hell and death from the devil.
> I believe that you preached to the spirits in prison, that you rose from the dead on the third day and ascended back to heaven where you now intercede on my behalf.
> Lord, I accept your sacrifice for me. Come into my life and rule it. Lord, I'm asking you for deliverance today. I'm sorry for all my sins. I count your enemies my enemies.
> Lord, I know that you require me to forgive every person and because you have asked me to do it, I do so now.
> I forgive every person, living or dead who has ever harmed me, talked behind my back, hurt me, or tried to dominate or control me.
> I forgive them freely and permanently, just as much as I'm asking you to forgive me.
> Lord, I'm sorry for every activity of the occult that I have ever been involved in. I renounce every form of it

in which I have participated, those named and those not named here:

Ouija board
Séance
Horoscope
Fortune Telling
Wizardry
Palm Reading
Magic
I renounce them all, Lord Jesus.
I hate them.
I turn against them.
I resist them.
I repent of them.

And now Lord, I hereby resist the Devil:

Satan, I hate you!
I renounce you!
I resist you!
I hate all of your evil works!
I command you to loose your hold on me,
in the mighty name of Jesus!
I charge you to depart and come out,

In Jesus' mighty name!
You have to go!
I claim the merit of the blood of Jesus Christ against you!
I adjure you in the name of the Lord to depart now!
I expel you now! Amen.

MINISTER'S INSTRUCTION:

Now, begin to firmly expel from deep down. Expect the evil spirits to begin moving out! This is what you have come for. Do not hesitate. I will come by, ready to assist you as the Lord leads. Do not believe the devil's whispering lies and deceptions. Persist until you have your miracle - right here and now. Prayer warriors begin to exercise your Holy Spirit gifts on behalf of those in need, even while they read this book. We are family- the family of God. Now, Lord, thy will be done here on earth, as it is in heaven. Amen.

10

INTERVIEW QUESTIONS AND ANSWERS

1. Tell me about your book. What is it about?

Answer: Book One is the first of our trilogy which together reveal the ongoing warfare between the invisible forces of God and those of Satan. Explained are its cause from the beginning until now, and its purpose to settle their dispute over freeing enslaved humanity. Typical battles are exemplified in ten cases of deliverance from demons. I personally ministered in nine of the ten, and two are in extreme detail of demons and the minister responding in human languages in their battles. Each case is both testimonial and a resource for teachers to encourage others to engage to win their personal battles.

2. That sounds exciting

Answer: Indeed it is!

3. Do you find that people actually believe there are – as you say – invisible agents of evil?

Answer: Many do, others do not. But everybody agrees that bad things occur to cause pain, anguish, and death. Jails, hospitals and graveyards are full to overflowing with victims who could not answer why their calamity happened to them. Newscasters report all the bad stuff but cannot tell us the reason for it, even questioning what motivated the perpetrators.

4. Are you convinced that the answers you provide are legitimate?

Answer: The first 37 years of my life were devoid of answers to misery. Over the next 50 years, however, answers came progressively as tormenter demons were cast out of me. That revelation changed my life so dramatically that I pursued it with zeal. In a similar way I have helped others. There are multiple surface causes, but the origin of all of them is the same. Evil is not a principle but the person of the Devil. Jesus said that we should pray, "…deliver us from *the evil one*" [Luke 11:4].

5. How did your personal help come about?

Answer: When a doctor, psychologist, and psychiatrist were unable to help I finally turned to the Holy Bible to find an answer. Since I didn't have one to read, I stole one out of a motel room in Michigan and read it avidly for two years. I was astonished to learn that Jesus could actually raise the dead! I couldn't get away from it. I found that this was the answer. Since that time my study of the Scripture has been the basis and rationale for the way I have lived and for writing these books.

6. If someone owns a Holy Bible to read, why would they need or want your book?

Answer: Obviously, the Bible is the primary source for everyone. But it is so comprehensive that its many parts need to be taught with emphasis and clarity. It contains unlimited thousands of messages. As the title of our book suggests, there are two literal, invisible kingdoms operating at the same time and in the same place, at war with each other. Both seek the loyalty of their adherents. While the Holy Bible describes them, we confirm them with contemporary testimonies that prove the Bible is the ultimate authority. Apart from it I have nothing to offer.

7. Many people regard all this as science fiction. What would you say to them?

Answer: Yes, you are right. That is exactly what I thought at first. As it turns out, however science fiction actually originates out of the two literal, invisible kingdoms at war with each other. The remarkable thing is where you find them. Jesus explained that "The kingdom of God is within you" (Luke 17:21). Now don't get mad when I tell you that the *other* kingdom is there also! The character and symptoms of both are described in Galatians 5:17-21. Our trilogy of books expands terse bible facts in cryptic detail to show readers how to be victorious "… over all the power of the devil " (Luke 10:19).

8. Why does it take three books to cover one subject?

Answer: Actually, it was written to be one manuscript for a single volume. But editor Terry Lea decided it covered too much for only one, so she broke it into three. I guess she thought I was *the man who wrote too much.* As she edited, I kept on writing, until she told me to stop writing! Her assessment was correct. It takes a lot to convince folks to believe what seems unbelievable. It is a stretch to tell them that battles rage first inside the mind, before they destroy the body through disease and death.

9. Would you classify this as a book of theology? What practical use does it have?

Answer: It is less than Jesus taught, but is only theological in practical, miraculous demonstrations. He healed the sick, raised the dead, opened blind eyes, and cast out demons. This book teaches the same things in Jesus' words, but emphasizes a side of spiritual warfare that most have neglected to teach. It is practical in showing others how to do the same things one-on-one that Jesus did. It does not discuss miraculous so much as it *is* miraculous. It also is prophecy, and history of the past, present, and the future, with little talk and much action.

10. Where is your book offered for sale?

Answer: Wherever books in print or eBook are sold. Amazon is the primary distributor both direct and in store; Special pricing applies for bulk quantities, especially for evangelists and missionaries.

RECOMMENDED DELIVERANCE RESOURCE OUTLETS

DEREK PRINCE MINISTRIES
P.O. BOX 19501
Charlotte, NC 28219 USA
www.derekprince.org/fyp
(800) 448-3261

50 Books written by Derek Prince. Cassettes, CD's, DVD's, Streaming MP3. Brilliant teaching on most Bible subjects. Pioneer in deliverance.

IMPACT CHRISTIAN BOOKS
332 Leffingwell Ave.
Kirkwood, MO 63122 USA
www.impactchristianbooks.com
(800) 451-2708 or (314) 822-3309

Publisher, bookstore, distributor. Books, DVD's. Broad subject variety – many titles on the subject of deliverance.

LAKE HAMILTON BIBLE CAMP
Merrill Miller
P.O. Box 21516
Hot Springs, AR 71903 USA
www.lhbconline.com
72LHBC@cablelynx.com

DELIVERANCE-THEME BOOK TRILOGY

**War of the World, Flesh, and the Devil
Book One, Book Two, Book Three**

Order individual title or as a trilogy set, directly through Amazon.com or through local bookstores.

Trade discounts are offered to individual buyers of multiple copies, and to volume buyers such as churches, leaders of home-meetings, bookstores, distributors, and libraries.

Missionaries and evangelists may acquire these books at deep discounts to use as premiums or as a fundraising gift offer. CD's and DVD's may follow.

License to republish in national languages may be available under contract for single book title or for the trilogy of books – in print or e-book.

www.ingramcontent.com/pod-product-compliance
Lightning Source LLC
Chambersburg PA
CBHW052025070526
44584CB00016B/1904